Teaching Life Skills
to Children and
Teens With ADHD

A GUIDE FOR PARENTS
AND COUNSELORS

Vincent J. Monastra, PhD

AMERICAN PSYCHOLOGICAL ASSOCIATION

WASHINGTON, DC

Published by
APA LifeTools
750 First Street, NE
Washington, DC 20002
www.apa.org

To order
APA Order Department
P.O. Box 92984
Washington, DC 20090-2984
Tel: (800) 374-2721;
Direct: (202) 336-5510
Fax: (202) 336-5502;
TDD/TTY: (202) 336-6123
Online: www.apa.org/pubs/books
E-mail: order@apa.org

In the U.K., Europe, Africa, and the Middle East, copies may be ordered from
American Psychological Association
3 Henrietta Street
Covent Garden, London
WC2E 8LU England

Typeset in Sabon by Circle Graphics, Inc., Columbia, MD

Printer: Gasch Printing, Odenton, MD
Cover Designer: Berg Design, Albany, NY

The opinions and statements published are the responsibility of the authors, and such opinions and statements do not necessarily represent the policies of the American Psychological Association.

Library of Congress Cataloging-in-Publication Data

Monastra, Vincent J.
   Teaching life skills to children and teens with ADHD : a guide for parents and counselors / Vincent J. Monastra, PhD. — First edition.
      pages cm
   Includes bibliographical references and index.
   ISBN 978-1-4338-2099-1 — ISBN 1-4338-2099-4 1. Attention-deficit hyperactivity disorder. 2. Attention-deficit disorder in adolescence. 3. Life skills—Study and teaching. I. Title.
   RJ506.H9M653 2016
   618.92'8589—dc23
                                                  2015019978

British Library Cataloguing-in-Publication Data
A CIP record is available from the British Library.

Printed in the United States of America
First Edition

http://dx.doi.org/10.1037/14798-000

Teaching
Life Skills
to Children and
Teens With ADHD

To God, from Whom all wisdom comes.

CONTENTS

Teaching
Life Skills
to Children and
Teens With ADHD

INTRODUCTION

I'll never forget the moment when I first became a dad. The feeling of sheer terror that my son would not survive childbirth was quickly replaced with the amazement of being part of creating a new life. The next couple of days at home for me were just a blur of "final" preparations. Then came the real moment of departure: bringing my son home from the hospital. Three-day-old Reuben was all cuddled in, not a care in the world, and about 5 minutes into the ride home with me and his mother, reality hit me. No more nurses showing me how to feed him. No one who could translate baby cries into "I'm hungry," "I need a burp," "I'm cold," "I need a hug," "I'm tired," or "I'm wet and poopy." I thought, "What in the world do I do with this little guy?"

Of course, instinct kicked in, and I eventually learned how to give my little guy what he needed. Even though those first few weeks and months are exhausting, most babies handle entry into the world just fine, and so do we. We're reassured when they seem comfortable and content and figure out pretty quickly what they need when they start to fuss. We take a bazillion pictures to document every moment in their physical development and settle into our various versions of family life.

Time goes by, and before we know it, our babies are heading off to nursery school or preschool. All of a sudden, their little prince and princess habits need to be toned down a bit. Those temper tantrums they throw at home to get their way start to show up at school. Their tendencies to ignore Mom and Dad's directions don't disappear when they show up at "Future Leaders of America Nursery School." Their inability to share becomes a focus for concern. That high energy that they used to be able to wear out on their little trikes bubbles out all over the rug at circle time.

Even more bewildering is the total change of rules when they transition from preschool to kindergarten. During their preschool years, they were encouraged for talking and playing with other little kids. Then they head into kindergarten, and it's no longer "OK" to do that in the classroom. Being a "helper" in my two youngest sons' kindergarten class was a real eye-opener. At times I could feel frustration mounting and the tension in the air as I watched little boys and girls get corrected whenever their eyes were not on their own work, when they were talking with others, when they were touching anything but what was in front of them, and when they got out of their seat to visit with a buddy in their class. All of this was OK in preschool. Who changed the rules?!

For most kids, these are just momentary glitches. Parents and teachers are able to teach and encourage preschoolers and kindergarten students how to act in social situations. Most will learn within a few months how to handle this new world. They learn to pay attention when the teacher talks and follow directions in the classroom. They can focus on their work for the 10 or 15 minutes required and get most of it done. They learn how to make friends, figure out how to share, and handle those moments when they feel frustrated without saying mean things, biting, or hitting other kids. They experience small measures of success and newfound friendships—life is pretty good.

However, some children don't learn these lessons so easily. No matter how many times a parent or teacher says, "Look at me when I'm speaking," the child continues to look everywhere else. No matter how many times a parent or teacher tells a child to sit still, stay in line, use "inside voices," or share, change just doesn't come. No matter how many times they tell a child to stop grabbing and pushing, they still find themselves pulling the child off of other kids. These children don't seem to understand words such as *boundaries* and *personal space* and are constantly being corrected for being "hyperactive" and "impulsive."

For other children and teens, the issue isn't about being restless, impulsive, or overly active. Instead, the problem for these children is that they don't pay attention very well unless they are involved in doing something they like. These are the kids who can't remember to bring home their assignments but can remind you that you promised to take them shopping a week ago (and give you the exact time, exact place, and your exact words). These are the kids who give up on practicing their spelling words or math problems in 30 seconds but could play Minecraft, build with LEGO® bricks, watch TV, ride their bikes, or skate for hours. These are the kids who couldn't follow through on a simple instruction such as "Please put away your dishes" but could give you detailed instructions about how to succeed on a video game or operate your smartphone, tablet, or other electronic device. About 5% of our children have a degree of inattention, impulsivity, or restlessness at home or school (or both) that doesn't ever seem to get much better because they have something called attention-deficit/hyperactivity disorder (ADHD).

DOES YOUR CHILD HAVE ADHD?

If you are uncertain if your child has ADHD, take a couple of minutes to complete this checklist that provides the core symptoms of ADHD. For a child or a teenager to have ADHD, they need to show at least six symptoms of inattention, and/or hyperactivity and impulsivity, for at least 6 months. Here are the symptoms of ADHD as listed in the diagnostic manual used by physicians, psychologists, social workers, and other mental health counselors (*Diagnostic and Statistical Manual of Mental Disorders, Fifth Edition;* American Psychiatric Association, 2013).[1] Check if the problem described is a cause of concern to you.

Inattention

My child has problems[2]

_____ paying close attention to details and makes careless mistakes in school tasks, work assignments, or other activities

_____ sustaining attention in tasks or play activities

_____ listening when spoken to directly

_____ organizing tasks and activities

_____ engaging in tasks that require sustained mental effort (like school or homework)

_____ with losing things that are necessary for tasks or activities

_____ with distractibility

_____ with forgetfulness

Number of symptoms of inattention: _____

---

[1] For counselors and therapists reading this book, as of October 1, 2015, for billing purposes, mental health professionals are required to use the latest version of the World Health Organization's diagnostic coding guidelines, laid out in the *International Classification of Diseases*, or ICD. For more information, see http://www.apa.org/international/outreach/who-icd-revision.aspx.

[2] Checklist from *Diagnostic and Statistical Manual of Mental Disorders* (5th ed.), by the American Psychiatric Association, 2013, Washington, DC: American Psychiatric Association. Copyright 2013 by the American Psychiatric Association. Adapted with permission.

Hyperactivity/Impulsivity

My child has problems

_____ controlling fidgeting with hands or feet; is squirmy

_____ with leaving seat in the classroom or other situations in which remaining seated is expected

_____ controlling the urge to run about or climb excessively when it is inappropriate

_____ playing or engaging in leisure activities quietly

_____ controlling the urge to talk excessively

_____ controlling the urge to blurt out answers before questions have been completed

_____ waiting turn

_____ controlling the urge to interrupt or intrude on others

_____ with restlessness

_____ with excessive activity; is on the go or seems "driven by a motor"

Number of symptoms of hyperactivity/impulsivity: _____

If your child has shown at least six symptoms of inattention, six symptoms of hyperactivity/impulsivity, or both for 6 months or longer, and these problems seem to be happening more often than they do in other kids their age, then there is reason for you to wonder about a possible diagnosis of ADHD.

WHEN DID THE SYMPTOMS BEGIN?

The next question to ask yourself is: "When did these problems begin?" Parents of a child or teen with ADHD will almost always recall that they started being concerned about their child's attention, impulsivity, or restlessness by the time the child was 12 years old.

If symptoms began by that age, it is another indicator that the child has ADHD.

WHERE ARE THE SYMPTOMS OCCURRING?

Children and teens with ADHD won't have problems paying attention in just one situation. Although children who are inattentive but not hyperactive may not be rated as having an unusual number of symptoms in all settings, it is rare for a child with ADHD to show some symptoms in only one place. The child who is having problems paying attention to instructions, following directions, or controlling behavior at home is also likely to be having similar problems at school; at an after-school activity; or at an evening dance, gymnastics, karate, scouting, or sports program. If your child is having some problems of inattention and/or impulsivity and hyperactivity in more than one setting, then you have another reason to wonder about a diagnosis of ADHD.

ARE THE SYMPTOMS BEING CAUSED BY OTHER MEDICAL OR PSYCHOLOGICAL PROBLEMS?

The next step for you would be to meet with your child's physician and begin the process of medical and psychological evaluation to determine whether your child truly has ADHD. For example, at my clinic, nearly 33% of children have been found to have a vitamin D deficiency or insufficiency, which can cause symptoms of inattention and mood problems. Another 25% have learned that they have undiagnosed visual problems (e.g., visual tracking and convergence disorders) that make it difficult for a child to pay attention while reading, writing, and completing math problems. Even though the lessons in this text have helped children with and without ADHD, my experience is that unless the medical causes of a child's symptoms of inattention, impulsivity, and hyperactivity have been identified and treated, their ability to learn life skills will be hampered. So take the necessary steps to make sure that your child is accurately diagnosed and treated before beginning this program.

FOCUS ON SKILL DEVELOPMENT

Checklists listing symptoms of ADHD naturally focus on what's going wrong, which is helpful in figuring out if a child has a condition like ADHD. My perspective is that treatment for children and teens with ADHD needs to go beyond symptoms and focus on what skills we want our children to learn. To help you with this task, I've also included one other checklist that you might find helpful, whether you're raising a child with ADHD or are a counselor, health care provider, or educator interested in teaching life skills at your school, office, or clinic. The "Functional Assessment Checklist: Home Version," at the end of this chapter, provides a way to help you get a comprehensive picture of the kinds of skills that a child may need to develop. After you've taught the lessons in this book, you can use the checklist again to get an idea of which lessons have been learned and which still need to be developed. Some parents, physicians, educators, and counselors find it helpful to determine a "score" indicating their child's level of functioning. To that end, I've included a copy of the "Interpretation Guide for the Functional Assessment Checklist: Home Version" for you to use as well.

WHY I WROTE THIS BOOK

When I began my career as a clinical psychologist, I was asked to pitch in and try to help children and teens who had ADHD. I quickly realized that I didn't have much to offer. To be honest, most of what I had been taught simply did not work with kids who kids who had ADHD. Even though I was uncertain how to best help these children, I was certain about one thing: These kids had grabbed my attention and my heart. It was true that many of these children would come into my clinic and either have nothing to say or have a lot to say about nothing that seemed important. And yes, these were the kids who couldn't remember to brush their teeth in the morning but could remember what mom or dad promised 3 days ago. They were the kids who'd get uncontrollably furious over some disappointment, but get over it in 15 minutes, even though their parents couldn't. These were the kids who wanted to have friends, but hardly anyone wanted to hang out with them. At recess time, they just stayed by themselves or ran around in circles. No one invited them over for play dates; rarely were they invited to birthday parties.

Despite all these problems, I couldn't help but be drawn to the enthusiasm and talents of these kids. Even though they'd be bored out of their minds on the baseball field, they could do amazing tricks on their bikes or skateboards; become black belts at age 10; and amaze people with their dancing, dramatic, or musical ability. These were the kids who couldn't figure out their multiplication tables but could build a replica of Captain America out of LEGO pieces. These were the kids who struggled so hard not to become the "Child Left Behind" in school but ended up believing that they were just stupid and had no real future simply because they could not master advanced mathematics, figure out the meaning of some metaphor in an obscure poem, remember two semesters of historical trivia so that they could pass state examinations in global studies, or write a three-page paper on *The Catcher in the Rye*. These kids were highly creative, intelligent, and talented but simply didn't succeed at schoolwork. I became determined to help them find a way to develop the skills they needed to develop friendships, a sense of purpose, and confidence.

During the past 20 years, I have dedicated myself to trying to understand what was going on physically with these children and teens. After all, how could children who could pay such great attention on some things be so unable to focus on schoolwork? I used a kind of brain scan (a quantitative electroencephalogram, or EEG) in my research and learned a lot about the behavior of the brains of children of ADHD. As a psychologist, it was a great feeling to see so many parents express relief and excitement as they watched a brain scan provide information about the neurological symptoms of ADHD in their child. After evaluating thousands of children and teens, my model for the diagnosis and treatment of ADHD was published by the American Psychological Association in the book *Unlocking the Potential of Patients With ADHD: A Model for Clinical Practice.*[3]

What I learned during those decades was helpful in guiding certain parts of the treatment of my patients. However, I was left with the feeling that I had dedicated my time to helping kids improve their attention without ever focusing on what was really important for them to learn. At first, I worked with the parents of children at our clinic to try to figure out the kinds of parenting techniques that seemed to help teach and motivate children to learn new skills. This research proved quite productive and led to the publication of our award-winning parenting program, presented in the first two editions of my book *Parenting Children With ADHD: 10 Lessons That Medicine Cannot Teach.*[4] However, even though the parenting program helped at home, my patients still seemed to have a lot of social problems at school and other situations.

So we took life skill instruction one step further. Because my patients and their parents knew that many of their problems involved other people, we needed to find a way to teach and practice life skills with others. We recognized that even if children could learn how to have conversations with their parents, they still had to learn how

---

[3]Monastra, V. J. (2008). *Unlocking the potential of patients with ADHD: A model for clinical practice.* Washington, DC: American Psychological Association.
[4]Monastra, V. J. (2004). *Parenting children with ADHD: 10 lessons that medicine cannot teach.* Washington, DC: American Psychological Association.
Monastra, V. J. (2014). *Parenting children with ADHD: 10 lessons that medicine cannot teach* (2nd ed.). Washington, DC: American Psychological Association.

to have conversations with kids their age. We realized that even if a child felt loved by his or her parents, there were other sources of confidence that involve experiences not all parents can provide. Most important, we were aware that many of the children avoided involvement in group activities. We feared the long-term results of this isolation and felt compelled to act. We knew that we needed to go "beyond attention."

What emerged over the next decade was a life skills program that could be taught in homes, schools, clinics, and ADHD support groups. In our program, groups of parents and children work together to establish friendships and a social network and to learn essential life skills. Because we recognized that learning any new skill requires ongoing practice, one of the key components of my clinic's program has been the establishment of communication networks between parents so that each child would have about 10 to 15 new friends with whom they could have fun and practice skills between classes. In the first meeting, kids and their parents share phone numbers and e-mail addresses and arrange to get together between classes. One of the most fulfilling parts of my involvement in the program occurred when I had the chance to listen to kids describe what they had done with their new friends between classes.

WHAT'S IN THIS BOOK

This book describes our clinic's Life Skills Program and how you can develop essential life skills in children at home; at school; or in a support group for parents, grandparents, and other care providers of children and teens with ADHD.

The book is set up so that you can get a feel for what it is like to be part of a life skills class. Just like I do at my clinic, I start each chapter by talking about the problem we're taking on and the life skill that you'll be learning. Then there are exercises to teach, model, and practice these skills. At the end, there is a challenge activity related to the skill being taught in which kids and their parents or other care providers have fun competing for prizes.

Like the program offered at my clinic, this book begins with a lesson on healthy diet, sleep, and exercise habits. That's because hungry, tired, and out of shape kids don't learn anything very well. The same is true for kids who have other kinds of medical problems that can cause attention problems (e.g., anemia, hypoglycemia, diabetes, thyroid disorders, and allergies, as well as deficiencies of vitamins D and B, calcium, zinc, and magnesium). For that reason, every child who participates in our Life Skills Program has been screened for such medical problems before they begin our classes, and we emphasize healthy eating, sleeping, and exercise habits throughout the program.

The next series of lessons focuses on building confidence. We concentrate on improving confidence through learning skills that matter to other kids, facing fears, developing friendships, and acting in a way that matches the child's moral code. We also teach children how to join social groups, engage others in conversation, and respond to peer rejection and teasing. The program also includes lessons on problem solving, organizational skills, and developing "emotional sensitivity" (i.e., showing appreciation, kindness, and generosity). Although teaching organizational skills would seem to be a lesson that some parents would like us to take on earlier in the program, I've found that the development of friendships with the other children in the group is enhanced by focusing on helping children "team up" to face fears, try out new activities, and practice conversational skills. For that reason, the lesson on organization follows those targeting confidence building.

In this book, you will find practical strategies for teaching each of these life skills. You will also learn ways to make the lessons interesting and fun. One of the most fundamental lessons I've learned is that kids with ADHD will pay attention if what they are seeing and hearing comes across as important, interesting, or fun. So each

13

lesson in this book contains two parts: a presentation of the lesson intended for parents, counselors, teachers, or other group leaders and a worksheet to be used with the child or children participating in the group.

HOW THE LIFE SKILLS PROGRAM WORKS AT MY CLINIC

To help sustain interest and the attention of kids, I have found it helpful to divide each class into four parts. Initially, I encourage groups to have pizza or some other kind of easy finger food for a light snack. This reduces anxiety and sets the stage for practicing conversation skills in a common setting (i.e., while eating with peers). At our clinic, we set up small seating arrangements for groups of three or four parent–child pairs. While they munch, each child is encouraged to describe one way that he or she practiced the skill from the previous lesson in the group. Group leaders circulate around the room to ensure that each child participates in this part of the program. We require parents to accompany their child to class and stay with the child for the entire session. One reason for parent presence is that it helps to keep kids focused, on task, and engaged. It also helps parents learn what we are teaching so that they can continue to practice and reinforce lessons at home.

Next, the day's lesson is presented. These are brief presentations, and each child is given a worksheet to follow along with their parent. The group leaders demonstrate the skills described and then guide parents and kids in the practice exercises. Because children with ADHD will quickly tune out if the leader is boring, it is important to remember that lessons have to be presented in ways that are lively and engaging. The group leaders need to find ways to make the lessons interesting and fun while getting across the benefits of trying out the new skill. Kids with ADHD are built to tune out the uninteresting, unimportant, and nonfun aspects of life.

Following the guided practice time, there is a group competition in which some aspect of the day's lesson is developed into a game in which parent–child pairs compete with each other for a prize (cash, tickets to a movie, gift cards for bowling, passes to the zoo, nearby science center, etc.). Finally, we review the homework for the coming week, discuss ways to inspire kids to practice, and make sure that kids are paired with others for home practice and end the meeting.

HOW YOU CAN TEACH LIFE SKILLS USING THIS BOOK

If you are not planning on teaching your child these life skills in a group, then I'd recommend that you set up a time each week for teaching and practice. Usually, there's more time on the weekend than during the week. If you anchor the time around a meal, you can begin with eating and then shift into a conversation about the life skill that you'd like your child to practice and learn in the coming week. If you have other children, you'll probably find that they will want to join, and it's often worthwhile to include them to help practice the lessons being taught. You'll also discover that it's helpful to set up goals for your other children to accomplish each week, even if they don't have ADHD. This way, your child with ADHD doesn't feel like he or she is the only one in the family who needs to work at "getting better." Kids also like it when their parents share some of their goals for the week so that they can learn from them how to set out and achieve a personal goal.

If you are interested in reading scientific papers on any of the topics that I talk about, consult the Supplemental Resources section at the end of the book. I've arranged the resources by lesson to make it easier for you to find what you're looking for. I've included a couple of sources that can provide more detailed information. From my perspective, the best resource to learn about the scientific research on ADHD or on any topic is to search on PubMed. This online library was developed and is maintained by the National Institutes of Health and gives you access to more than 23 million scientific studies. PubMed can be found online at http://www. ncbi.nlm.nih.gov/pubmed. Just type in the key words about the topic that you want to learn more about, and you're on your way to a world of information. The Supplemental Resources section also includes some websites that you might find interesting and informative.

Teaching Life Skills to Children and Teens With ADHD was written so that you could teach the lessons we've learned at my clinic in your home and your community. Although a parent, grandparent, or other guardian and a child could use this book alone, I encourage you to pair up with other parents who have a child with ADHD to get the most out of this experience. Counselors, mental health providers, or local ADHD support groups (e.g., Children and Adults With ADHD: http://www.chadd.org) can use the information contained in this book to establish Life Skills groups in their schools, clinics, and practices. By teaming up with others, you will be able to establish a group of friends for your child. Such social networks will become crucial as children proceed through the middle school and high school years.

As you read, you'll find that many chapters contain checklists, worksheets, or both. I included these as tools for reflection, teaching, and engaging children and teens in learning life skills. Some of them take the form of quizzes; others are more like a guided journal entry. They're designed to help your children (or the kids in your Life Skills group) develop new habits and patterns of behavior that will make them more successful in life, both during their school years and when they hit adulthood. If you are working with a group, you might want to download and photocopy some of the worksheets. To do this, go to http://pubs.apa.org/books/supp/monastrateaching. The worksheets are not for commercial use. If you would like to repost or use the worksheets in any format, please obtain written permission from APA's permissions office, or, where indicated on the worksheet, from me, at the FPI Attention Disorders Clinic (http://www.drvincemonastra.com; e-mail: dr.vincemonastra@gmail.com).

WHEN TO GET PROFESSIONAL HELP

ADHD is not a condition that is easily "fixed." Even though stories shared on the Internet may suggest that a child with ADHD was somehow magically "cured" by a particular medication, dietary supplement, attention training program, counseling approach, or other helpful intervention, no treatment takes care of all of the various kinds of problems experienced by a child or teenager with ADHD. Children and teens with ADHD are often talented, quite smart, and wonderfully engaging and creative people. However, every child who has been diagnosed with ADHD will experience some type of dif-ficulties learning how to succeed at home, at school, and in the community.

You and I both realize that your child is able to do some things very well. You and I also know that if your child has ADHD, there are a number of skills that he or she needs to learn. Some of the lessons that you'll try to teach will come easily. You'll read a lesson in this book, try out the approach that I'm sharing with you, and your child will get it right away. However, other times you'll try to teach your child, but it will be really hard for him or her to learn.

For example, some of my patients really struggle with the textures of foods, and so it is difficult for them to eat enough protein. Although I mention several strategies to overcome this kind of problem, you might find that nothing is working. Consultation with your child's physician, a nutritionist, or a mental health professional who is familiar with eating problems may really help you find ways to "desensitize" your child to these new textures and improve his or her diet.

Other children and teens that I work with really have a hard time controlling their emotional reactions. Some are so fearful that they won't try anything new. They'll just want to hang out at home and play their electronic devices, asserting that "everything else is boring." Although I've included strategies to help these children break out of their shell, consultation with a mental health provider who is familiar with behavioral therapy techniques (such as exposure therapy and in vivo desensitization) may prove helpful too.

Problems with depression and anger outbursts can also be hard for some of my patients to overcome. The lessons that I teach in this book may be enough to help children learn how to calm down, get focused, and figure out how to get what they want. However, if the suggestions in the book do not seem to be working, consultation with your child's physician and a mental health professional will be needed.

Conversations also can be difficult for children and teens with ADHD. Again, I hope that the suggestions and exercises I describe in this book will be a great way to begin to turn this around. But if your child is making little headway as you work through the exercises in this book, it may be useful for you to seek help from a speech-language therapist to work on what are called *pragmatic language problems*. That's a fancy name to describe the speech or language problems that a child is having with day-to-day conversations and social interactions.

The bottom line is that every child or teenager with ADHD needs to be working with a knowledgeable physician, mental health provider and other specialists who realize that successful treatment for patients with ADHD takes more than a 15-minute monthly medication checkup or a weekly, unfocused 30-minute play therapy session in which the child and therapist hang out and play some type of board game or electronic game, while the therapist asks "How's it going at home? How's it going at school?" If that's what is happening with your child, I'd encourage you to consult with a professional who is well versed in the treatment of ADHD and can work with you to systematically teach the types of skills covered in this book.

Even though it will take time to build the skills taught here, now is the time to start. Every day that children experience the pain of social rejection, the humiliation of academic failure, and the sense that they aren't loved because all they ever hear is that they're doing something wrong, they become more convinced that life is hopeless. Too many children have reached that conclusion, with tragic results. So let's begin.

Functional Assessment Checklist: Home Version

Child's Name: _____

Name of Rater: _____

Relation to Child: _____

Date of Rating: _____

Children and teens diagnosed with ADHD can have a wide range of problems at home. To develop a comprehensive treatment program to best help your child and to evaluate your child's progress, I would like you to complete this brief checklist. Please read each statement and write a numerical rating from 1 to 5 (or write N) using the following scale:

1. Rarely or never
2. Once or twice per week
3. Three or four times per week
4. Almost daily
5. Every day
N. Not expected at this age.

INDEPENDENT LIVING SKILLS:

____ Wakes in the morning, without repeated prompting

____ Washes, brushes teeth, combs hair, without repeated prompting

---

(continued)

Functional Assessment Checklist: Home Version (*Continued*)

_____ Gets dressed in the morning without repeated prompting
_____ Makes bed in the morning without repeated prompting
_____ Eats breakfast that includes some kind of protein without repeated prompting
_____ Takes medication without repeated prompting
_____ Remembers to pack homework, school papers without repeated prompting
_____ Gets to the school bus (or car) on time in the morning without repeated prompting
_____ Eats a lunch at school that includes protein
_____ Comes home after school on time
_____ Does homework without repeated prompting
_____ Does at least one "chore" without repeated prompting
_____ Eats a dinner that includes protein without prompting
_____ Puts away clothes, toys, papers, etc., without repeated prompting
_____ Uses a calendar, phone, computer, or other device to keep track of their schedule
_____ Cleans room without repeated prompting
_____ Washes up, brushes teeth in the evening without repeated prompting
_____ Goes to the bedroom at bedtime and rests quietly without repeated prompting

_____ **Total: Independent Living Skills**

SCHOOL FUNCTIONING:
Please read each statement and write a numerical rating from 1 to 5 (or write "N") using the following scale:

1. Rarely or never
2. Once or twice per week
3. Three or four times per week
4. Almost daily
5. Every day
N. Not expected at this age

Functional Assessment Checklist: Home Version (*Continued*)

_____ Gets to classes on time
_____ Brings the necessary books and materials to class
_____ Remembers to turn in homework
_____ Sits in seat at school
_____ Does not interrupt the teacher
_____ Speaks when called on in class
_____ Does school work in class
_____ Copies down homework assignments
_____ Remembers to bring home books and materials needed for homework

_____ **Total: School Functioning**

EMOTIONAL CONTROL:
Please read each statement and write a numerical rating from 1 to 5 (or write "N") using the following scale:

1. Rarely or never
2. Once or twice per week
3. Three or four times per week
4. Almost daily
5. Every day
N. Not expected at this age

_____ Follows parent instructions without arguing
_____ Solves disagreements with siblings and parents without arguing or fighting
_____ Controls physical outbursts of anger (e.g., throwing/hitting objects; striking people)
_____ Controls verbal outbursts of anger (e.g., insulting, yelling, threatening others)
_____ Apologizes, accepts responsibility for mistakes, and makes up
_____ Handles disappointment without sulking, complaining, or crying
_____ Attempts activities that cause anxiety

_____ **Total: Emotional Control**

(continued)

Functional Assessment Checklist: Home Version (*Continued*)

SOCIAL SKILLS:

Please read each statement and write a numerical rating from 1 to 5 (or write "N") using the following scale:

1. Rarely or never
2. Once or twice per week
3. Three or four times per week
4. Almost daily
5. Every day
N. Not expected at this age

_____ Does something kind and thoughtful for another family member

_____ Tells a story about their day during meal time

_____ Listens to other family members tell stories about their day

_____ Asks questions that are on the topic when listening to other family members

_____ Shares toys, games, and other playthings without complaint

_____ Spends time reading, painting, building, playing a musical instrument, or engaging in any recreational activity that requires thinking (*not* video/computer games)

_____ Calls/contacts another child to talk

_____ Is called/contacted by another child to talk

_____ Invites a friend to get together

_____ Is invited by a friend to get together

_____ Joins and participates in an organized community social group (e.g., sports, scouts, dance, music, drama, church group, 4-H Club, or other group)

_____ **Total Social Skills**

© Vincent J. Monastra, PhD. Reprinted with permission.

Interpretation Guide for the Functional Assessment Checklist: Home Version

The evaluation of functional impairment is a requirement for determining a diagnosis of attention-deficit/hyperactivity disorder (ADHD) according to the *Diagnostic and Statistical Manual of Mental Disorders, Fifth Edition*.[5] The Functional Assessment Checklist: Home Version (FAC:H) provides the perspective of a parent, grandparent, or other caregiver on the functional abilities of a child in grades K to 12 in the following categories: Independent Living Skills, School Functioning, Emotional Control, and Social Skills. Raters provide an assessment of the frequency of targeted behaviors, using a coding system ranging from 1 (*Rarely or never*) to 5 (*Every day*). For interpretative purposes, scores are summed and averaged within each category. An overall impairment index is determined as well.

SCORING:
Parents or other caregivers are requested to respond to a total of 45 questions, using the following rating system:

1. Rarely or never
2. Once or twice per week
3. Three or four times per week
4. Almost daily
5. Every day
N. Not expected at this age.

Next, the ratings are summed for each category and averaged, providing a category rating ranging from 1 to 5.

Finally, the averaged ratings for each category are summed and a cumulative average is determined.

[5]American Psychiatric Association. (2013). *Diagnostic and statistical manual of mental disorders* (5th ed.). Arligton, VA: Author.

(continued)

Interpretation Guide for the Functional Assessment Checklist: Home Version (*Continued*)

INTERPRETATION:

Because the FAC:H provides an assessment of the frequency of targeted behaviors at home, the following classifications are used to describe degree of functional impairment:

CATEGORY/CUMULATIVE IMPAIRMENT RATINGS:

1.0 to 1.49: Severe Impairment

The child has been rated as "rarely/never" demonstrating skills that would be expected in a school-aged child.

1.50 to 2.49: Moderate Impairment

The child has been rated as demonstrating skills that would be expected in a school-aged child "rarely/never" to only "once or twice per week."

2.50 to 3.49: Mild Impairment

The child has been rated as usually demonstrating expected life skills from "once or twice per week" to "almost daily."

3.50 to 5.00: No Impairment

The child has been rated as usually demonstrating expected life skills "almost daily" to "every day."

© Vincent J. Monastra, PhD. Reprinted with permission.

SUCCEEDING IN LIFE ISN'T EASY, BUT IT STARTS OUT SIMPLE: EAT, SLEEP, AND EXERCISE

Chances are, you've heard that it's important for children to eat nutritious food, get a good night's sleep, and exercise every day. You probably know that our kids are supposed to be eating something more for breakfast than a bowl of cereal, getting to sleep before 10:00 p.m., and exercising something other than their fingers. The problem for many of us is that we have busy work schedules and hectic lifestyles. The truth is that a lot of us don't seem to have enough energy or time in the day to get all of the household chores done, make sit down dinners, shuffle our kids to all their after-school activities, and wrap it all up so that *we're* asleep by a decent hour. So how do we make this happen for our children? How can we make the commitment for change? Let's take a look at your child's eating, sleeping, and exercise habits and think about how we can find ways to improve.

EATING WELL WHEN THERE ARE SO MANY WAYS TO EAT POORLY

At my clinic, the number one concern of my patients' parents (aside from their children's inability to focus) is that their children don't eat well. Some kids don't eat. Some kids only eat carbs. A much smaller group of kids actually eat healthy meals that contain a combination of protein, carbs, fruits, and veggies.

There are several types of poor eaters who come to my clinic. None of them is eating enough at breakfast to have any chance of paying attention during the day. See if you can identify your child in one of these five categories. The first group is my *Exhausted Kids*. These are the children who stay up so late watching TV, playing electronic games, tweeting, texting, or checking their Facebook status and e-mail, by the time they finally fall asleep, it's well after midnight, and there is simply no way they feel like eating breakfast.

The second group includes my *Body Conscious* tweens and teens who eat little during the day because of their fear of gaining weight and not being able to squeeze into their skinny jeans. So they skip breakfast and think that having a few bites of a salad and a Diet Coke constitutes a big lunch. Although by the time dinner rolls around they feel pretty hungry and will have a fairly balanced dinner, their eating habits do not provide sufficient protein for them to be able to pay attention during the school day. Unlike children with eating disorders, these children are weight conscious, but they maintain a weight that is within expectations for their age.

The third group of poor eaters include my *Picky Eaters*. These kids never seem to experience hunger. They will sit at the table, looking bored and uninterested in their food. After being coaxed into taking a few bites, they let their parents know that they're "full," or their "tummy hurts," or they'd rather hang upside down by their toes than eat. These same kids will eat like little banshees when their parents "give in" and let them have foods from their favorite food groups (sweetened cereals; crackers with jelly; or other high-carb, low-protein offerings). However, like the other groups of poor eaters, they are not eating sufficient protein at breakfast and lunch to sustain attention during the school day.

Then there are my *Distracted Eaters*. These children get so distracted at the table that they either run out of time for their meal, or their parents run out of patience. Even when parent desperation causes mothers to take away one of their children's toys to get them to focus on eating, without skipping a beat, the children find creative ways to occupy their hands instead of eating. They'll build bridges with their spoons and forks, they'll use their napkin as a trampoline for Cheerios, and if all else fails, exchange farting noises with their brother.

The last category of my poor eaters are my *Carb Addicts*. This group includes children who fill their tummies with spoonfuls of crunchy things that are dyed with colors not found in nature. Or the children who move so slowly in the morning that there's simply no time to feed them much more than a toaster strudel, a frozen waffle, a cereal bar, or anything else that can be grabbed on the way out the door.

Rarely will I get the chance to work with kids in the *Well-Fed* category. These kids eat a balanced breakfast that includes protein-rich foods like eggs, some meat, and a glass of milk, along with some carbs like a waffle, an English muffin, some oatmeal, a low-sugar/high-fiber cereal, or a bagel, as well as some fruit like orange juice or a banana. Only these kids have a fighting chance of staying full and focused all morning long.

WHAT MAKES A GOOD BREAKFAST AND LUNCH?

One of my earliest memories as a kid was breakfast time. Even though my mom was a great Italian cook, breakfast was pretty basic. It usually consisted of a bowl of cereal (Cheerios to be exact—can't let little Vinnie have too much sugar). I can still hear the commercial telling parents to give their kids the "Pow, pow, powerful, good, good, feeling of Cheer, Cheer, Cheerios." Like a lot of little kids, I was fed a bowl of cereal, given a glass of milk, and sent off to school with my big sister (to make sure that I didn't get too distracted on the way and forget to go to school). So I was one of those "Carbs" kids.

Now, stoked up with that big bowl of cereal, I was supposed to have the firepower to handle pretty much any school task all morning long. It didn't turn out that way. Like clockwork, between 9:00 and 9:30 a.m. every day, I felt a deep emptiness in the pit of my stomach. I was hungry, and I was having a hard time paying attention. All I could think about was that yummy meatball sandwich that my mom had packed away in my lunch bag. If I was lucky, there were a couple of double fudge, chocolate-striped cookies, which I hoped hadn't gotten squished by the apple in my bag.

Even though I had no scientific understanding of the relationship between breakfast composition and attention, I knew firsthand that my morning meal of Cheerios wasn't cutting it. You see, if children have just cereal for breakfast, they've been given enough fuel to last them about 1.5 to 2.0 hours at school. That's it. Unfortunately, for most kids, the cafeteria fill-up doesn't come for about 4 hours. So if all your child has for breakfast is a bowl of cereal, a piece of toast, a toaster strudel, or some other carbohydrate, he'll run out of mental energy long before he gets to lunchtime.

Even though that's not good, it's still a lot better than my Non-eaters. Unfortunately, the kid who skips breakfast is lost. There is no way that she'll be able to sustain attention during the morning. In fact, she'll start to feel fatigued and inattentive within 45 minutes of being awake. Compared with kids who eat cereal for breakfast, the breakfast skippers will be outperformed by the "cereal eaters" on pretty much any measure of attention and memory for about 4 hours.

The kids who have a clear advantage are my Well-Fed kids, who consume a breakfast that has a combination of protein and carbohydrates. This kind of breakfast provides carbs to give us a burst of mental energy and the protein needed for the creation of those brain chemicals (neurotransmitters) that our brain needs to sustain attention and concentration. I still remember the picture on the cereal box when I was growing up that showed how cereal was part of a "complete" breakfast. That picture showed two eggs, a couple strips of bacon, toast, milk, orange juice, and that bowl of Cheerios. Somewhere during the past few decades, that picture got blurred.

Nowadays, we hear that we can get full and focused by eating some square wheat cereal. That's a classic half-truth. It is true that the square wheat cereal eaters will feel full and be more focused than the breakfast skippers. But they will consistently get beaten on tests of attention and memory by the complete-breakfast eaters. And, as noted, the complete-breakfast eaters will have the ability to sustain attention and memory for about 4 hours, long enough to make it to lunchtime. The other kids will fade.

The same process holds true at lunch. If your teenage daughter is uncomfortable eating lunch or your 6-year-old son is too distracted to eat, then she or he will have difficulty sustaining attention in the afternoon. I can't even begin to estimate the number of teenage girls I have treated who ate a few fries from their boyfriend's tray or a salad at lunchtime and were exhausted, irritable, and famished by the time they got home. Or the number of children with attention-deficit/hyperactivity disorder (ADHD) who are so distracted by the noise and activity level of the cafeteria that they forget to eat. Or the number of children with ADHD who have no appetite at lunchtime and are off the wall by the time they get home after school. Bottom line: unless you help your child figure out a way to eat enough protein at breakfast and lunch, he will not do as well as he could in school and will present many more problems when he arrives home.

So what is enough protein? Not as much as you might think. For children ages 4 to 10, at least 10 grams of protein at breakfast and at least 10 grams at lunchtime are enough. For children ages 11 to 14, 20 grams at each of these meals is sufficient. For boys ages 15 to 18, at least 25 grams at each of these meals is sufficient (for girls, at least 20 grams at breakfast and lunch is recommended). Part of a comprehensive treatment plan for children with ADHD is to help them eat a complete breakfast and lunch. To get a better idea of what a complete breakfast meal looks like, check out ChooseMyPlate.gov. On this website, you'll learn how protein is used to build muscle, brain chemicals (neurotransmitters), and other structures; how fats are used to build the coating around brain cells that help them work faster; how carbohydrates provide a burst of energy for every cell in the body; how vitamins are like little construction workers, manufacturing antibodies and other essential life substances; and how minerals provide the missing ingredients in thousands of body production processes and help transport nutrients throughout the body. Without good nutrition, the child with ADHD will not be able to sustain attention, concentration, and behavioral control during the day, regardless of the type of medicine that he or she is taking.

To help you figure out what you should feed your child at breakfast and lunch when it comes to the protein, I'd recommend using the Rule of Sevens. About 7 grams of protein can be found in the following foods:

- 1 ounce of beef, pork, poultry, or fish
- 1 ounce of cheese (a slice of cheese pizza has about 10 grams)
- 1 egg
- 7 ounces of milk (fat content does not matter)
- 2 tablespoons of peanut butter

WHAT TO DO IF EGGS AND OTHER HIGH-PROTEIN FOODS MAKE YOUR KID QUEASY

Some kids really struggle to eat traditional breakfast foods like bacon and eggs in the morning. Let's talk about some strategies that we can use to get protein-rich foods into your child at breakfast and lunch.

The first clue is that the breakfast and lunch meals have to include something tasty or pleasurable. I recall reading about a study in which rats were able to make a choice between pressing a bar that would deliver a little bit of food to them or a bar that would provide electrical stimulation of pleasure centers in the brain. Guess what happened? The rats chose the pleasure bar until they starved to death. If we want to turn breakfast time around, we need to find ways to make meal time more pleasurable for our kids, as well as a priority for even our body-conscious ones.

The first discovery is to find out what kinds of protein foods your child likes to eat. A lot of my patients absolutely can't stand the sight or smell of eggs. But when I start talking to them about the foods they really like (e.g., peanut butter and jelly, pizza, pot pies, chicken nuggets, meatballs, hot dogs, grilled cheese, ham and cheese sandwiches, smoothies, milk shakes), or some of the light, easily digestible Greek-style yogurts, the tasty protein bars (Special K Protein Bars, Gatorade's G-3), or even some of the high-protein cereals (Special K Protein Cereals, Cheerios Protein Cereal) a light bulb goes off, and they begin to realize that breakfast can be yummy and pleasurable. So a breakfast of a peanut butter and jelly sandwich would have about 14 grams of protein from the 4 tablespoons of peanut butter, and anywhere from 4 to 12 grams of protein from the bread. Add in an eight-ounce glass of milk (with 8 grams of protein), and you've gotten a substantial amount of protein in a simple breakfast meal.

Of course, nothing is easy for some of my Noneaters. Even if you come up with foods they like, they'll still avoid eating. For those kids, making breakfast fun requires more than just pleasant-tasting foods. These kids need to be engaged at breakfast, otherwise they just won't eat. For these kids, breakfast time might need to include a game. This could be a card game like Uno, a simple game of Connect Four, or any game in which players take turns. The child needs to eat a bit of food before each turn.

For teens, the idea of playing a game with Mom or Dad likely isn't going to light up their pleasure centers. But taking the time to talk with your teen and stocking up on some foods that she likes for breakfast is one way to make some headway. And the payoff for your teen is that she'll feel a lot more awake in school and maybe she'll have your permission to head off to school with that smartphone, go to a friend's house after school, or use her screens when she comes home after school.

The big challenge for you as a parent is to break through with a breakfast that your child will eat that has enough protein for his age, as well as carbohydrates. This is a must-win situation, but it doesn't have to be a battle. The goal is for you and your child to figure out meals for breakfast and lunch that are yummy or at least tolerable. Along the way, you'll pick up on basic nutrition facts—the importance of protein, how to identify high- and low-protein foods, and figuring out some breakfast and lunch meals that will work for your child—that help everyone in the family, not only the one(s) with ADHD.

PUTTING YOUR CHILD'S BRAIN IN SLEEP MODE

Sleep is important when it comes to attention. For some parents, getting their kids to go to bed is no big deal; for many others, it's an event to be dreaded. The fact is, a lot of children with ADHD have a really hard time settling down to fall asleep. It could be because they haven't eaten enough protein early in the day, so their brain's manufacturing plant for melatonin (the chemical that puts us to sleep) is running behind. Maybe the child has been out practicing soccer; swimming; karate; or participating in some type of church, school, or community activity until 7 or 8 p.m. Or maybe he has been spending the hours before bedtime watching exciting television shows, playing video games, or socializing with friends on his cell phone or the computer. Whatever the reason, lack of sleep at night is one of the leading causes of inattention and irritability in children (and grown-ups too), whether or not they have ADHD.

The reason that getting sufficient sleep is particularly important for children and teens with ADHD is that they already have one condition that will make it hard for them to pay attention. ADHD alone will cause them to have difficulty listening to their teacher, following directions, remaining on task while doing seatwork, and having the mental energy to stick with it and finish their homework. ADHD combined with another medical condition that will reduce their attention and memory is a double whammy that your child really doesn't need.

How much sleep is actually needed? Well, for adults the research is pretty clear. Adults who get less than 7 hours of sleep will have problems paying attention; remembering important things (like where they put the car keys); being calm and rational when their child is forgetful, distracted, impulsive, and so on; and solving day-to-day problems more creatively. Kids who don't get enough sleep will have the same problems. For children in the elementary grades, 10 to 11 hours per night is recommended. Middle school and high school students would benefit from getting at least 9 hours of sleep. However, because many middle and high school students need to be at their school bus stop before 7 a.m., that's pretty hard to do. If you can find a way to get your teenager to bed by 10 p.m., you're doing pretty well.

How to make that happen can be tricky. Here are some ideas. First, eating a breakfast and lunch that contain protein is important for more than just attention during the school day. It also helps with falling asleep at night because the protein you eat in the morning, in addition to giving your body the tyrosine it needs to make brain-awakening neurotransmitters like dopamine, noradrenalin, and adrenalin, also gives your body the tryptophan it needs to make the "put you to sleep" neurotransmitter melatonin that helps you fall asleep at night.

The second key to falling asleep has to do with exposure to bright lights. We have a specific body part, called the pineal gland, that manufactures melatonin from the protein we eat during the day. However, this gland only goes to work in the dark. Before the days of televisions, high-intensity video games, and computer screens, it would get dark outside, the pineal gland would make a batch of melatonin for us, and we'd fall asleep pretty close to sunset. Nowadays, we create an indoor world that is as bright (if not brighter) than the sun, create high-definition video worlds that get our adrenal glands pumping, and shut down our pineal glands. As a result, we struggle to fall asleep.

One way to treat this problem is to shut down the various screens in your home about 1.5 to 2.0 hours before your child is to go to bed. That means smartphones, too. Within that time frame, you and your child could read together, play a nonelectronic game, work on a puzzle or build LEGO® bricks, draw, or color. I know that kind of stuff is pretty old school, but it works.

Another option that some parents consider is the use of a melatonin supplement or medication to promote sleep onset. Giving a child 1 to 3 mg of melatonin about 1.5 to 2.0 hours before bedtime can be helpful. After a couple of weeks of this supplement, your child should have a better appetite in the morning and you should be able to discontinue the supplement. For children who are hyperactive and irritable at night, medications such as clonidine, guanfacine, and Intuniv (a time-release version of guanfacine) can also be helpful. These medications help tone down the adrenaline system and reduce restlessness and anger. If you have been unable to establish healthy sleeping habits by changing diet, evening activities, and melatonin, use of such a medication would merit consideration. Like all medications, there are side effects with the use of clonidine, guanfacine, and Intuniv that should be discussed with your child's physician.

It's hard to change sleeping habits by offering some type of reward or threatening to take something away. Although some parents might have a little bit of success by developing a point system that rewards a child for staying in bed or telling a child that she won't be able to play video games tomorrow if she doesn't get to bed, that's not a winning strategy for most of the parents I know. You'll probably need to look at your child's breakfast and night-time routines. Kids who do not eat protein at breakfast often have a hard time falling asleep at night. In part, that's because the pineal gland isn't getting any of the protein it needs to make that "fall asleep juice" (melatonin) until lunch time (or later). Without protein, the brain simply can't make the chemical foundation that helps us fall asleep at night. So one part of changing sleep patterns involves making sure that your child eats protein at breakfast.

A related issue involves food consumption at night. Because of the busy schedules of parents and kids, many children and teens will eat late dinners (6:30–7:30 p.m.). If a child is loading up on a big meal at 7:00 p.m., there is no way he'll be able to fall asleep by 8:30 p.m. That would be like putting logs on a campfire and wondering why the fire won't go out. If you won't be able to have a family meal until you get home at 6:30 p.m., it's better for your child to have their dinner after school (3:30–4:30 p.m.) and have a fruit and cereal snack with you at 7:00 p.m. Finally, many kids will have caffeinated drinks or foods (remember chocolate is a stimulant) in the evening. It's a good idea to avoid those.

Next, think about your child's evening routine. When the sun goes down, the pineal gland begins to convert the neurotransmitter serotonin into melatonin. However, as I mentioned before, the pineal gland only makes melatonin in darkness (low-light situations). This was no big deal in the pre-electricity days. Sun goes down, darkness is everywhere (except some dim light from a fireplace, candles, or lanterns), and people fell asleep pretty early.

Now, many homes are equipped with large, bright, high-definition televisions that show an image as intensely lit as sunshine.

A lot of homes have these mini-suns in nearly every room of the house. In addition, most people prefer to watch shows that stimulate the release of dopamine and adrenaline, two brain chemicals that wake us up. Many homes also have computers with equally bright screens, streaming images from millions of websites into our homes. Each of these electronic portals seeks to engage us by showing us scenes that cause the release of dopamine and adrenaline. Toss in the various personal communication devices (smartphones) and websites (Facebook, Twitter, etc.), as well as amazingly fascinating and stimulating video games, and it becomes pretty clear that children (and adults) have a wide range of activities that can keep them up for hours instead of falling asleep.

To help children and teens fall asleep, I recommend that families set up a simple rule: All screens are turned off 1.5 hours before bedtime. During this time, I encourage families to have a simple snack (like a low-sugar bowl of cereal, milk, fruit), read together, or play a nonelectronic game as a family. Family Game Night doesn't have to be only on Saturday night, and a good book can be every bit as enjoyable as a video game. If you don't have any idea which books might really engage your children, ask the librarian at your child's school or the public library. They can let you know their favorites and also give you a list of the books that have won awards for being the best in children's literature (Caldecott Medal, Newbery Medal). For families that are trying to promote their child's relationship with God, this is a good time to read and reflect on the Bible, the Torah, the Koran, or other inspirational books.

HOW TO GET 'EM MOVING

For some kids with ADHD, exercise is a nonissue. They have an abundance of energy, are in near-constant motion, and can get a cardio workout while running in place at the kitchen table. However, for other kids diagnosed with ADHD, exercise is torturous, at least at first. They'd much rather come home; grab a bag of chips or cookies; head to the television, computer, or video-game system; and settle in for hours of sitting while accomplishing amazing feats of skill, albeit virtual skill.

Unfortunately, the brain and the body know the difference. Even if you singlehandedly destroy the enemy in Call of Duty, outscore Lebron James on an NBA Xbox game, or lead the Eagles to the NFL Championship on Madden's EA Sports Football game (I'm still waiting on the real-life version of that fantasy), in reality, nothing has happened. Your muscles weren't working (not unless you count button pushing to be a workout). Your heart and lungs didn't get any stronger. And while you were playing, chances are you weren't refueling your body. In the end, you feel drained, irritable, and uninterested in doing pretty much anything else at the end of your 4-hour stint of game playing.

So what is *exercise*? Basically, exercise happens when our large muscle groups are moving at a rate that gets our heart pumping faster than usual for somewhere between 20 and 30 minutes. How much faster is needed? Here's a simple way to calculate the exercise heart rate zone. First, subtract the person's age from 220. Multiply that by 0.6. This would be the threshold (i.e., minimum) heart rate for exercise. So if you have a 10-year-old child, you subtract her age from 220 (which is 210), multiply that by 0.6 (which is 126), and that would be the minimum heart rate for her exercise program. You'd next determine the upper limit for heart rate (i.e., the ceiling, beyond which could lead to cardiac problems) by subtracting her age from 200 (you'd get 190). Multiply that by 0.8 (you'd get 152). So the exercise heart rate zone for your 10-year-old is between 126 and 152.

Why exercise? There are numerous scientific studies that point out that exercising for 20 to 30 minutes at least 3 days a week improves attention, concentration, and problem-solving ability and reduces depression, irritability, and anxiety. So exercise gives you a pretty good return on the investment. How can you help your kids get started? My rule of thumb is that my patients need to be involved in some type of group physical activity three times per week. This could be gymnastics, karate, dance, running, skiing, or more traditional sports such as baseball, football, basketball, hockey, tennis, soccer, or lacrosse. Most kids enjoy these activities (provided they don't have an overly aggressive coach who believes that winning is the sole purpose of sports and losing is the end of the world).

However, some kids with ADHD are uncoordinated and, because of that, aren't very interested in sports. For these kids, I've found that high-activity games on the Wii (the movement ones, not the push-the-button ones) are great starters. Trampolines are also winners. Adventure hiking (not walking around the block) can also captivate kids. Joining scouts, 4-H, and other groups can promote this. Swim lessons, joining swim teams, karate classes, working 1:1 with a trainer at one of the baseball, soccer, football, or lacrosse (for example) academies that are sprouting up everywhere, or scheduling time with a physical therapist who can develop and (more importantly) encourage physical skills are other ways to get started.

Can't get the kids out of the house? I'm guessing that everyone in the family could use a little workout. If that's the case, you might want to try linking TV, electronic game, or computer time with 20 minutes of exercise. The deal is pretty straightforward. To hop on the computer or video game or watch a favorite show, we need to get in 20 minutes of exercise first. If you happen to have a treadmill, elliptical, exercise bike, free weights, abdominal machines, or whatever, great! If you don't have any exercise equipment, here are a couple of exercises that you could consider.

To make it fun, do it with your children and challenge them to beat you. To make it a little more motivating, tell them that if they can do better at any of these tasks than you, you'll let them stop the exercise and return to playing their favorite game. This forces you to get in shape too!

1. Push-ups: Lie on the floor in prone position (belly down), perched on your toes. Place your hands to the sides of your body at shoulder width or slightly wider. Then, push your torso and legs off the floor by extending your arms. Lower the body by bending the arms at the elbows. For correct alignment, imagine a straight line running from your head down to your ankles. (If you need to modify the exercise, especially when first getting started, you can do a push-up on your knees, rather than your toes, but still keep a straight line from the neck down the torso to the hips.) Move up and down as many times as you can. Then shift to the next exercise.

2. Plank: Lie on the floor, again in prone position. Place your forearms on the floor at your side, aligning your elbows and shoulders (looking a little like the Egyptian Sphinx). Then push your body off the floor (again perched on your toes), engaging the core by sucking in your belly. Try to keep your back as straight as possible (like a plank of wood); your body should form a straight line from shoulders to ankles. Hold this position for as long as you can. Then shift to the next exercise.

3. Superman: Lie face down on the floor. Extend your arms out in front of you as far as you can. Lift your arms and legs off the floor and point your toes backward, forming an elongated "U" shape. Hold that position for as long as you can. Then shift to the next exercise.

4. Sit-ups: Lie flat on your back on the floor. Pull yourself up to a sitting position (without using your hands). Some people will reach down and touch their toes. Others will bring their knees up and touch their knees with their elbows. Do this as many times as you can. Then shift to the next exercise.

5. Run in place: This translates to a jog without going anywhere. Turn on the TV, music, or whatever and jog along for the remainder of the 20-minute workout period.

6. Jump rope: This one is not just for little girls. A lot of athletes train with jump ropes to build cardiovascular health as well as increase core body strength.

TIPS FOR TEACHING GOOD EATING, SLEEPING, AND EXERCISE HABITS

When I teach life skills at my clinic, I'll give each child a worksheet that explains the lesson in a simple, straightforward way. The kids will use the sheets during the class and take them home to remind them of the lesson and to keep track of how they are doing. You can go online to http://pubs.apa.org/books/supp/monastra-teaching to download the full worksheet. It includes a summary of the information in this chapter and a quiz on the protein content of foods. It also includes a log for recording how many days a week the child ate breakfast and lunch, exercised, and slept for the optimal number of hours for his or her age group. The quiz and log are shown in the following exhibits.

TRY A CHALLENGE GAME

If you're teaching life skills in a group format, try ending your meeting with a game or activity to make the lesson a bit more fun. For example, you might use a little tabletop basketball game where you

Test Your Food IQ

How well do you know your foods? Compare the two foods listed on each line and circle the one you think has more protein.

Column A		Column B
Bowl of a toasted oat cereal (Cheerios)	or	Slice of pizza
Grilled cheese sandwich	or	Hot dog
20 peanuts	or	1 apple
6 chicken nuggets	or	1 egg
6 fish sticks	or	1 quarter pound hamburger
Small bag of potato chips	or	1 small bag of cheesy puffs
1 cup of baked beans	or	8 oz yogurt (not Greek style)
1 small beef taco (6 oz)	or	3 pancakes
1 egg	or	3 tablespoons peanut butter
2 slices of French toast	or	1 cup of shredded wheat cereal
Protein bar (e.g., Special K®)	or	2 blueberry cereal bars (Nutrigrain®)
1 cup of spaghetti	or	1 cup of sliced oranges

Note. Answers are at the end of the lesson.

fling a little ball into a net and the ball goes out the other side to your partner. Or place a Nerf® hoop on the door and shoot into the hoop. Have a competition in which parent–child teams compete against one another to see who can hold a plank exercise the longest. Other games could include trashcan basketball or creating paper airplanes and competing to see which family's plane will fly the longest or fly into an object (e.g., trashcan). You could even add a prize such as a

Worksheet for Life Lesson 1: Keeping Track of Your Eating, Sleeping, and Exercise

You can make this chart as simple or detailed as you want. For example, you can check the boxes to show that you ate breakfast and lunch, or you can write down what you ate for your meals or how many grams of protein you ate. For exercise, you can aim for once a week if you're not exercising at all right now or try to get moving 5 days a week if you now exercise only two or three. You could also write down the number of minutes and/or name of the activity you did. For sleep, aim for 9 hours or the recommended number of hours for your age.

Challenge	Monday	Tuesday	Wednesday	Thursday	Friday	Saturday	Sunday
Breakfast (Protein)							
Lunch (Protein)							
Exercise (Minutes)							
Sleep (Hours)							

gift card to a pizza parlor, video game arcade, movie theater, bowling alley, or other recreational center. If you teach life skills at home, consider dividing the family into teams; the losing team can make a meal or dessert for the family.

POSITIVE PRACTICE, POSITIVE PUNISHMENT, AND TIME STANDS STILL

So what happens if the child doesn't do her challenge or life skill homework for a particular day? Instead of takeaways (e.g., No watching TV after school because your child didn't eat protein at breakfast), I've found it far more effective to use Positive Practice, Positive Punishment, and Time Stands Still. Each of these strategies is described in detail in my book, *Parenting Children With ADHD: 10 Lessons That Medicine Cannot Teach,* 2nd ed.[1] Here's a brief description of each of these techniques and how you could use them for this lesson.

Time Stands Still is a strategy that essentially puts a child "on hold" for not doing "the right stuff." For example, the child who refuses to exercise needs to know that until he exercises, he does not have your permission to play anything. When your children resist doing the right stuff, they know it's not OK. And when we do something that's not OK, we need to stop, do the right thing, do something to make up for our "not so great choice," and then we're back on track. This is a pretty simple rule for any kid to learn. So the child who does not exercise needs to learn that until she does her exercise, her life is on hold. The child who does not eat breakfast needs to realize that his life is on hold until he eats his breakfast foods.

Time Stands Still is different from being grounded or having something taken away. When parents use this strategy, it's important to stress to their children that they are not grounded, they

---

[1]Monastra, V. J. (2014). *Parenting children with ADHD: 10 lessons that medicine cannot teach* (2nd ed.). Washington, DC: American Psychological Association.

haven't lost anything, and no one is taking anything away. The child is in a situation in which she needs to do the right thing for the "pleasure vault" (games, toys, TV, electronic games, smartphones, etc.) to open up. The longer you have to wait for your child to do the right thing, the more your child will need to do to "make up."

Positive Practice simply translates to requiring that children practice what they didn't do. The child who refuses to exercise is on hold until he does the 20 minutes of exercise that he's supposed to do. The child who refuses to eat her breakfast will need to eat a breakfast meal after school before she has your OK to get started on her after-school activities.

Positive Punishment is not like other punishment techniques. It does not involve yelling, threatening, or physically harming a child. There's nothing aggressive about it. Positive Punishment is a technique to motivate children that requires them to perform some type of action to make up for not doing "the right thing" in the first place. So in addition to having the child who skipped protein at breakfast have a breakfast meal after school (Positive Practice), I might have the child go into the refrigerator or cupboard and write down the protein content of a dozen foods (Positive Punishment). I might have him come with me to the supermarket and jot down the protein content of various foods. Then he'll need to tell me what protein-rich food he "promises" to eat for breakfast the next day. After completing those two tasks, he is free to play. The next morning, if he does not keep his word, we'll repeat this process after school, plus the child will have to do some other type of task to make up for not keeping his word.

I hope these strategies work for you, because to learn life skills, your child with ADHD needs to be treated for that condition and have a brain that is nourished, has plenty of oxygen, and is rested. If you are struggling to use the lessons in this section, don't be reluctant to share the information you're learning with your child's physician and therapist to see if they can help you make the changes that your child needs to succeed.

In case you were wondering, here's the answer key for Test Your Food IQ: B, B, A, A, B, B, A, A, B, A, A, A

MAKING YOURSELF HEARD BY STAYING CALM

Everyone gets angry sometimes. That's a simple truth. And when you were a little kid, your parents, grandparents, and other "teachers" tried to help you learn what to do when another kid took your toy, your mom or dad told you no, you had to do some chores when you'd rather play, or it was time for bed. So what did they teach you to do when you were starting to feel angry? Did they teach you to go to your room and pound a pillow? Did they give in to you when you had your little tantrums, teaching you that yelling works?

I'm asking these questions because of another simple truth: We can only teach what we've learned. In this lesson, we're going to focus on what you'd like your child to do when he or she starts to feel angry.

My clinic happens to be located one block away from Main Street in Endicott, New York. Like many "Main Streets" in the United States, there are easily a couple of dozen popular chain and local restaurants along the road leading to my clinic. Because many of the children who come for treatment are making the trip after school, they're kind of hungry. So a natural discussion in the car ride leading to the office is, "Mom, Dad, can we go to McDonald's (Burger King, Wendy's, etc.)?" Now, if the parents say, "Sure," then everyone's fine. But if Mom or Dad say, "No, not today. I packed a snack for you in the car," a huge problem can occur. I have seen kids who have been grounded for a month because of an emotional meltdown over being told no to a visit to McDonald's. These kids are so mad that by the time they've reached my clinic, their parents are embarrassed, as they sheepishly ask me if I could talk with their child in the car because he or she is refusing to get out and come into the clinic.

Kids with attention-deficit/hyperactivity disorder (ADHD) live in the extremes when it comes to controlling their emotional reactions. A lot of the time, it seems like nothing bothers them. They're pretty good at occupying themselves, which can be a problem in itself. Some will be perfectly content to go outside and ride a bike, swim, or play basketball or stay inside and watch television or play video games for hours and hours. But when you ask them to turn off the game and start their homework, or come in for dinner, or help you with a chore, it's the end of the world. Or if one of their brothers or sisters stands over their shoulders and watches them play a game, a fight breaks out. Or you tell them that they have to eat vegetables for dinner or have something more substantial for breakfast than a sugary toaster pastry or cereal, and they storm out of the room.

If that's happening in your home, you're not alone. In fact, the vast majority of children diagnosed with ADHD will also have other behavioral or emotional problems. Over the past 20 years, my clinic and other clinical research centers in the United States have been examining this problem. Here's what we know at this time. About 23% to 63% of children and teens diagnosed with ADHD will also have an oppositional defiant disorder. That means that a lot of kids with ADHD will argue and defy their parents, have problems controlling their anger, become quite irritable, and have difficulty taking responsibility for their actions. Another 20% to 50% of patients with ADHD will be excessively anxious and worried, have difficulty handling separation from their parents, need reassurance, be uncomfortable with the textures of certain foods or clothing materials, and have specific fears. A similar percentage will have a mood disorder and be depressed, irritable, moody, easily fatigued, and not feel like doing their homework or pretty much anything other than staring at a computer screen or their smartphone.

WHY DOES MY CHILD HAVE MOOD PROBLEMS?

I've seen so many instances in which kids have been diagnosed with multiple psychiatric diagnoses and their parents are feeling over-whelmed because nothing is working. So what's a parent to do? Well, the first step is to take your child to a physician who under-stands the big picture. This kind of physician will make sure that your child does not have one of about a half dozen medical condi-tions that can cause these kinds of emotional reactions. Kids with vitamin D deficiencies often have mood and attention problems that have nothing to do with ADHD or parenting style. So do kids who have allergies, anemia, thyroid disorders, hypoglycemia, sleep dis-orders, and other kinds of problems. Making sure your child doesn't have some kind of medical condition that will cause mood problems is a step that you don't want to bypass.

The second step is to understand the nature of the beast in a child. A child with or without ADHD will be more prone to lose his cool when he's hungry, tired, or lonely. So as you watch your child head into "grumpy land," review this simple checklist.

- Has my child eaten?
- Did he get enough sleep last night?
- Does he have friends and an active social life, or is he isolated and alone?

Remember, the tired, hungry, lonely version of your child is not a happy one. In Life Lesson 1, we talked about how eating a healthy breakfast and lunch, getting enough sleep, and exercising on a daily basis are the foundation of successful living. Now, we're going to focus on an equally important skill: learning how to calm down and focus when you are feeling mad, sad, or worried.

HOW TO GET YOUR COOL BACK IF YOU'VE LOST IT

Take a minute and think about what happens when you don't get your way. Say you wanted your child to stop playing a video game and start her homework. Maybe you started making your request calmly and patiently—you know, some version of "Honey, it's time to get started on your homework. Please turn off the game now." So far, you're calm, cool, and collected. There's been no change in your heart rate or breathing.

But after repeating the calm version of your request several times, you start to feel frustrated. Instead of yelling, you "stuff your feelings." Simply put, you close your mouth, stop breathing, and start to feel a new sensation: anger. Anger doesn't just pop up on its own. It's one of the emotional reactions that come when we stop breathing or begin to breathe rapid, short breaths. As soon as our breathing changes, our heart rate increases so that it can make up for the decrease in oxygen coming through the lungs. Blood pressure rises, and a variety of hormonal reactions occur as the body prepares for fight or flight, or freezes. We feel those physical changes as anger, anxiety/fear, or sadness.

Think about it. What happens to you when you get frustrated? Don't you stop breathing? I know I do. When it's about the fifth time that you ask your kids to turn off the TV and get to the table for dinner, aren't you becoming a little irritated? And when we're in a situation that scares us, our breathing changes too. We watch a horror film and are on the edge of our seat. As the scene unfolds and the vampire moves in for the kill, our breathing becomes shallow and our heart rate increases; we feel gripped with fear.

The same is true when we hear bad news and become "sad." Someone tells you that a neighbor's child has been hit by a car. If you care at all about the child, your breathing changes, your heart rate changes, and you feel sad. You get a call on the phone telling you that you did not get selected for a job that you hoped would turn your life around. Again, there are changes in heart rate and breathing that come before the feeling of sadness.

Because these physiological changes trigger our change in mood, controlling them is at the core of any effort to learn how to calm down. Most of us have heard various strategies to help. I can remember being told to "count to 10" as a child. I don't know about you, but when I'm mad, I can count to 10 pretty fast, so I never really felt the calm that was supposed to come when I did that. Other kids have been told to go to their room and pound their pillows or get in the shower and scream their lungs out. That may work better than counting to 10, but screaming as a way to calm down and pounding something aren't really the kind of strategies that carry over well into adulthood. Face it, by the time we're grown-ups, we're supposed to have learned something a little more refined than yelling, screaming, and sulking when life doesn't go our way.

So the first key in learning how to calm down involves changing your breathing and heart rate. The most direct and effective way to do this is by changing your breathing; change that, and the heart will follow. Here are a couple of strategies that can help.

1. *Take 10 big drinks of air*: When we stop breathing or start to breathe short, rapid, shallow breaths, the heart rate will speed up because the brain needs oxygen to keep working. The heart has to move whatever oxygen is available to the brain as quickly as possible. To change that, all we need to do is to find a way to drink in some air. Just like when we take a big gulp of a cool drink on a hot day and start to slurp down

51

the water, soda, or whatever, we can take a deep big gulp of oxygen. Most of the kids I work with know what it's like to take in a big drink of their favorite soda or other drink. They don't take a sip and put it down. They take a half-dozen or so big swallows.

So instead of counting to 10, learn to take 10 big drinks of air. For each drink, suck in as much air (through your nose) as you can and fill your lungs up. Then pause and let it all out through your mouth. Repeat this 10 times. By the time you get 10 drinks of air in your body, you're well on your way to calming down.

2. *Blow off steam*: Some kids have a hard time breathing in when they are mad. Their bodies are just too tense. So instead of drinking air in, they might find that it works better to try to blow air out. It sort of releases the "steam" inside them. For some kids, imagining that they are blowing out the candles on a birthday cake helps. For others, actually blowing up a balloon works well. The trick here is that every time you blow out a lot of air, your body immediately wants to take in some deep, long drinks. Your body does that for you naturally—you don't need to think about it at all. So after you blow off steam, you could try and see if you can slurp in 10 drinks of air.

After a child has gotten his breathing under control, it's time to get the brain into action. When we're angry, sad, or scared, our frontal lobe is pretty useless to us. We're not thinking about strategies to get what we want. For example, in that state, your child may be going over the greatest hits of how unfair Mom or Dad is, how his brother is such an idiot, or how much he hates the kids in his class. However, after we suck in a little air, the frontal lobe can get into the game.

WORKING YOUR OXYGEN-FUELED FRONTAL LOBE

The frontal lobe of the brain is pretty important when it comes to being strategic. Without air, the big part of our brain that helps us focus, think about our goals, and begin to figure out ways to get what we want is pretty much out of commission. Primitive fight-and-flight centers of the brain are getting fed the available oxygen, and so we are pretty good at saying mean things, pushing, hitting, threatening, or performing other angry actions. But once the frontal lobe gets some air, it can begin to ask two important questions:

1. What do I want?
2. What can I do to make it happen?

With oxygen, the brain can focus on answering these questions. Without oxygen, the brain will simply be gripped with anger, fear, or sadness—period! So once we drink in some oxygen, we can begin to take the next step in calming down: figuring out a way to get what we want.

I remember when I was a little kid. I tended to get pretty mad when I didn't get my way. In fact, I was a classic "head banger," long before any heavy metal band ever hit the stage. When I didn't get my way, I'd pound my head against a wall or grab and throw something, and storm out of the room. My parents were quite steadfast and never gave in, but it took me a long time to learn to do something else. Punishment might have taught me what my parents didn't want me to do, but I needed to be taught or discover what I was supposed to do.

I remember being a teenager and my dad was sitting with me trying to help me figure out what was the matter. I had gotten really angry over something stupid, and my dad was a pretty calm guy. So he's trying to figure out why I was furious about something so minor. He was this thoughtful dad, watching his kid go primitive over nothing, and he must have been thinking, "Wow, I wonder what happened to Vinnie at school today?" Well, after listening to my dad ask me some version of "What's wrong?" for the dozenth time, I said something sarcastic like, "Maybe I'd feel better if I just stood on my head." My dad said, "Hmm, why don't you try it?" So I did, and as the blood was heading to my upside down head, I began to calm down, and we both laughed about it.

It wasn't until I was in college and learned about this oxygen–anger connection that I figured out what had happened to me back then. Without realizing it, I had learned a way to get oxygen to the brain more quickly when I was angry: stand on my head. My grown-up version of this was to start taking gulps of air until my brain was ready to answer one simple question: "What do I want?"

This might seem like a no-brainer, but when people are angry, sad, or scared, you'd be amazed at what comes to mind when they ask themselves that question. At first, they might not have any answer, just a really strong feeling of anger or fear. Your child, for example, might find himself going over and over certain thoughts such as, "I can't believe Mom is such a jerk" or "I can't believe Dad is so stubborn." If that's what happens when he asks the question, encourage him to take in a couple more gulps of oxygen and try again.

When the child has enough oxygen going to his head, he'll be feeling calmer and may be able to answer the "What do I want?" question. He may be quite clear that he wants to go out with his friends or get that burger at McDonald's. He just doesn't know how to get there.

Which takes us to the second frontal lobe question: "What can I do to make it [my goal] happen?" Sometimes the answer to the question is for a child to ask her parents some version of "What's getting in the way?" The answer to the question is often a parent's fear or a need. Sometimes parents are afraid that something bad will happen if they say yes; sometimes they need something from the child before they can say yes. Either way, an important self-calming tool is for a child to learn to ask, "What do I want?" and then "What can I do to make it happen?" and then take some effective action, rather than yell, scream, pout, sulk, get moody, or stay scared.

Let's play out a couple of examples so that you can see how this works. What if you had a child who tossed her head back, yelled something angry at you, and stormed out of the room every time that she didn't get her way? Obviously, that's not a winning behavior. What do you do? Well, you could take away her electronic games to punish her for her actions, but that's likely to get her even madder, and it doesn't teach her what she's supposed to do.

In Life Lesson 1, I described how to use Positive Practice, Positive Punishment, and Time Stands Still to help your child begin to eat, sleep, and exercise. I hope you have found, or will find, some success using these techniques. Now your child has yelled at you and stormed out of the room because you told her she couldn't play on Xbox, use her phone, or surf the Internet. What now? What techniques work in this situation?

The first thing that's true is that your child's reactions are not OK. You know that, and so does she. The second truth is that you and your child now know that when we get mad, we aren't getting enough oxygen to our brains, so we will start to feel angry and want to say or do mean things. The third truth is that until we start to drink in enough oxygen to get our brain in the game, we're not going to solve anything.

Step 1 is for you, the parent, to take some deep breaths— enough so that you can answer the two frontal lobe questions ("What do I want?" and "What can I do to make it happen?").

Typically, your answers will be some version of: "I want my child to stop yelling, to breathe and calm down, to acknowledge that she just did the wrong thing, to apologize, and to do something to make up for her actions. After she does that, then we can talk about what's getting in the way of her being permitted to play her video games."

Step 2 is for the calmed-down version of you to head to your child's room and calmly remind her that she might want to suck in some air, and calm down, then head downstairs when she's calm and ready to apologize. The rest of the stuff (doing something to make up) and having a calm discussion to solve the problem can come *after* her brain (and yours) has enough oxygen.

Yes, there will be times that won't be your finest hour as a parent or grandparent, and you'll lose it. When the situation finally calms down, let the child know that you realize you should not have raised your voice and yelled. As hard as it is for anyone (even parents) to say "I'm sorry for yelling," it's the right thing to do. And your role is to teach your children the right thing to do, even when it's a little embarrassing for you. Modeling is a powerful way to teach a lesson to a child. As you're apologizing to them, reinforce the notion that "in our family, no one has the right to yell or scream at someone, and everyone, including Mom and Dad, will work on this so that we are a loving family, in good times and bad."

TIPS FOR TEACHING SELF-CALMING

I've found a couple of breathing exercises to be helpful to teach the oxygen–heart rate connection. The first breathing exercise that I like gets the heart pumping simply through movement. Take your pulse and figure out your heart rate while sitting and relaxing. Next, either run in place or stand up, sit down, stand up, sit down, stand up, sit down, about 15 times, then retest your heart rate. Typically, you'll find that your heart rate has gone up considerably and you are not feeling as comfortable as when you were just sitting quietly. Ask your child (or the rest of the group) to describe how it feels to have an elevated heart rate.

Another breathing exercise gets the heart pumping by holding our breath. This exercise mimics what happens when we get angry, scared, or disappointed. In this exercise, start by taking your pulse. Then hold your breath for as long as you can, breathe, and check your pulse again.

Once you and your child have played around a bit with these exercises, ask your child to think about something he wants and write it down. Maybe he wants permission to do something, or perhaps there's something he want his parents to buy. After he's done this, have him say what he wants out loud. Then you say no and deny him permission. Next, challenge your child to practice staying calm. Step 1: Establish breathing. Step 2: Start a conversation to figure out what's getting in the way and what he can do to make his wish a reality. If you are in a group, practice these self-calming skills together before heading home.

In my life skills classes, I'll usually play a game that involves breathing. Sometimes we do a "hold your breath" competition in which I ask each child and his or her parent to take one deep breath in and hold it for as long as they can. I'll mention how taking in deep breaths brings a lot of oxygen to the brain and that the better physical shape we're in, the longer we can last between breaths. We time the child and parent, and each family gets one Total Score. The family with the highest score wins a prize (e.g., tickets to a movie; coupons for a meal at McDonald's; passes to go bowling). Another game we sometimes use is balloon blowing. I'll pass out balloons to each child (all the same size, of course), and the child who gets her or his balloon to explode first wins.

To help children learn this lesson, I will give every family a copy of the practice sheet on the next page and review ways to calm down with them. I'll ask them to bring it back to the next class. I'd encourage you to keep track of each child's, or your own child's, progress this way too. It doesn't matter whether you are teaching your own child or are running a life skills class in your school, office, or clinic. I ask people to keep track of their self-calming practices for at least a 2-week period because once a habit gets established (and reinforced for 2 weeks), it usually sticks.

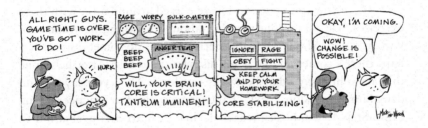

Home Practice Sheet

Face it, chances are something will come up this week, and you will get angry, worried, or disappointed. That will give you a chance to practice how to calm down. When you start feeling angry, worried, or disappointed, STOP, suck in some air and let it out (10 good breaths), and say nothing until you can answer these two questions:

1. What do you want?
2. What can you do to make it happen?

Remember, SAY NOTHING until you are breathing and you can answer these two questions. Once you're able to answer these questions, it means your brain is in gear, and you can go up to your parent (or whoever else triggered your reaction) and begin to work things out. How many times did you try breathing in and out instead of blowing up? Challenge yourself over several weeks to tip the balance toward calming yourself and staying in control. Put a checkmark in the box each time you do one of the following to help keep track:

	Breathed in and out 10 times	Calmed down	Figured out what I wanted	Talked it over and worked it out!	Blew up	Apologized and made up
Monday						
Tuesday						
Wednesday						
Thursday						
Friday						
Saturday						
Sunday						

GETTING WHAT YOU WANT IN LIFE WITHOUT GETTING INTO TROUBLE

The first conversation between a parent and child is a scream. At that instant, parents are relieved and overjoyed because their little baby has just said, "Hi, Mom and Dad! I just wanted you to know that *I'm alive*!" In the wonder, amazement, and fatigue of the moment, this strong burst of sound is so reassuring. There is no discussion about how to teach the baby a better way to express his or her needs. After all, he or she is "just a baby."

During the next 6 months, the baby learns to scream and cry when cold, hungry, or tired or when she needs a diaper change. She also learns that crying and screaming can get her a cuddle, a desired toy, or a favorite mobile turned on. Because she is just a baby, parents respond immediately—to the point of exhaustion. After all, it's important for the baby to realize that Mom and Dad are there to make sure that her needs are met and that this will happen "right away" (or pretty close to that).

So life goes pretty well (from the baby's perspective) until someone gets the bright idea that it is time for the baby to learn to do something other than scream to get what she wants. Without warning, how the world works changes dramatically for the child. Now if the child wants something, it's no longer OK to scream. Nope; to get that bottle, to get picked up, or for mom to come, the child will need to point or make some sort of sound to communicate a need. During this time, the child is taught to say something like "baa . . . baa" when she wants a bottle, "up, up, up" when she wants to be picked up, or say "ma-ma" or "da-da" to get a parent to attend to her needs.

Even though the child has to put up with a little bit of delay, the basic arrangement is still the same, which is: "If you need something, just let us know, and we'll take care of it for you." Pretty quickly, our children learn to say "baa . . . baa" or "ma-ma," and they usually get whatever they want. Sure, we stop them from swallowing LEGO® bricks, sucking on the dog's chew toy, or chucking their food off their highchair tray. But for the most part, we're trying to encourage our children to use words to express needs.

This type of arrangement typically continues until age 2 or 3. About that time, kids develop the strength and coordination to begin to explore the world and get things for themselves. Once we get to that point, the need to teach children how to get what they want in life without getting into trouble becomes a priority from a safety standpoint as well as from a life skills perspective.

During this early childhood period, parents teach a variety of behaviors. The child is taught to stop immediately when a parent says "no!" They are taught to say "please" and "thank you" to get what they want. They will learn to ask before the child leaves the parents' presence and to seek help if they want to reach an object that is out of easy reach. Crying and outbursts of temper become more of a concern beginning in the "terrible twos," and parents try to make sure that their child learns that crying or throwing a tantrum is not how people get what they want in life.

HOW "WHYNING" BREAKS US DOWN

If parents have done their job well, by age 4, children generally learn to stop crying and tantrumming when they don't get their way. By the time children enter kindergarten, "Whyning" begins to replace crying and tantrumming. Kids who become great Whyners learn to persistently ask "*Why?*" "*Why*, Mom? *How come*, Dad? *Why* can't I?" Although less dramatic than tantrums and tears, this "why . . . why . . . why . . ." can be pretty effective from a child's point of view. It disarms his parents, and he often ends up getting what he wants.

From my perspective, a child repeatedly asking "Why?" (when he doesn't get his way) is no different from a baby crying WAAHHHH; it's just cleaned up a little bit. Parents, teachers, and counselors need to help children learn that repeatedly asking "Why?" and Whyning won't work in the real world. Grown-ups generally hate to hear that Whyning, "Why–Why not" stuff. It's like nails on a chalkboard, and it really gets in the way of "getting what you want."

Unfortunately, tired, overworked parents get worn down by the incessant "Whys," tears, and tantrums that can occur at the end of their workday. As a result, they give in and provide the foundation for the development of a wide range of uncooperative behaviors, including ignoring and defying parents' requests, yelling and arguing with parents, and throwing objects or hitting parents when needs are frustrated. Such children do not limit their defiant behavior to home, and teachers are typically faced with the process of teaching such children cooperation and problem-solving skills in their classrooms. Typically, these children are quite aware about the "game" at play between themselves, their parents, and often their teachers.

I once had a conversation with a 9-year-old boy—let's call him Justin—whom I was treating for attention-deficit/hyperactivity disorder (ADHD). Justin had a brother who seemed to be the perfect child—Justin's brother seemingly did nothing wrong. He did not yell at his parents. When they asked him to help out with chores, he did them without hesitating or complaining. He did his homework without prompting, and he was earning good grades at school.

Then there was Justin. He did not listen to his parents' requests and nearly always gave them a hard time when they asked him to do something. He dragged his feet when asked to turn off the TV or video game, get dressed, or help out with chores. Homework time was a nightmare for his parents because Justin would just sit there and get nothing done unless they were with him. Even in their presence, he would complain and make their lives miserable until his parents left him alone in the room. Then he would start playing with whatever was nearby.

One day, I asked Justin (in his parents' presence, by the way) why he gave his parents a hard time and pretty much never did what they asked. I didn't ask the question in a mean or judgmental way. My basic approach to situations that I don't immediately understand is that even the most "crazy" behavior has a pretty good psychological explanation. So when I ask a question like this, I always figure that I'm going to learn something useful. Here's what Justin told me: "Doc, I don't do what my mom asks 'cause if you do what your parents ask, they'll just ask you to do more. Like my brother. He does everything they ask, and they just keep asking him to do more. Me, I don't do it, and so they just give up. Sometimes, they'll even ask my brother to do my stuff."

What could I say? It made perfect sense.

Needless to say, Justin's parents and I spent some time reviewing their lesson plan and revising their program at home. Basically, the sequence of "Get asked, balk, yell, resist, avoid, my parent gives up, I get to play, and they ask me to do less" was changed to "Get asked, do. If I balk, yell, resist, or avoid, my play will be interrupted until I apologize, do what I was asked, practice cooperative behavior at least three times (e.g., doing three chores the first time I'm asked), and then I have to do something nice for my parent to make up for the stress I caused in my home" (a more detailed description of techniques like Time Stands Still, Positive Practice, and Positive Punishment can be found in *Parenting Children With ADHD: 10 Lessons That Medicine Cannot Teach,* 2nd ed.).[1]

Once Justin was able to get in control of his uncooperative behavior, he and his parents were ready to take the next step in learning how to get what you want in life. Like the other children who have participated in our Life Skills Program, we started to teach Justin basic techniques that can change the no's in life to yesses. Basically, it's the kid version of Donald Trump's *The Art of the Deal.* That's what this lesson is all about. Learning how to get what you want in a way that will work in real life.

A WHINE-FREE WAY TO GET TO *YES*

Take a moment and think about what you do when someone says no to you. Let's say that you ask your supervisor to change your work schedule from second shift to first shift, and he says no. Let's say you ask your boss for a raise, and she says no. Maybe you want to visit your parents on Sunday, and your husband says no or "I don't want to." Or maybe you want to sign your child up for Pee-Wee football and your wife says no. What do you do then?

As you think about this, it's likely that you'll begin to realize that the same strategy you used when you were 8 or 9 years old is probably the one you'll use at 21 and beyond. If you grew up in a family where "no means no!" and you needed to "shut up" and "do what you were told—period!" chances are you'll react with anger and frustration, end up in a seemingly endless debate, or just withdraw whenever someone says no to you. Me, I learned a pretty neat strategy. It came from my dad and from watching good salespeople. It goes like this.

Whenever a person is told no, there are typically several reasons. If you reduce these reasons down to the basics, it translates to needs and fears. When a person says no to you, it is usually because of a combination of needs and fears. The key in turning a no into a

---

[1]Monastra, V. J. (2014). *Parenting children with ADHD: 10 lessons that medicine cannot teach* (2nd ed.). Washington, DC: American Psychological Association.

yes involves learning how to get the other person to define his or her needs or fears by conducting a needs–fears analysis. Once you have that information, you have the keys to "getting what you want." Here are a couple of examples.

I am often invited to give lectures to parent groups, educators, physicians, and mental health providers. This typically involves a plane commute and overnight stays away from home. It is difficult to get direct connections from my hometown in upstate New York to pretty much anywhere in the country, so it usually takes me at least 6 hours to arrive at my destination. I end up arriving in a city in the late afternoon and am transported to the speaking venue for my evening presentation. I have no car at that point.

One of the ways I demonstrate a needs–fear analysis during my presentations is to locate someone in the audience and ask that person for the use of his or her car for Friday and during my weekend stay in the city. At first these individuals think I'm joking. Anyway, after they realize that I am serious, they of course say no. I'll ask them some version of "What's getting in the way of you saying 'OK'?" At first, they might say, "I have to get home tonight." I respond "No problem. I'll drive you." They laugh, and I say, "So is it OK for me to use your car for the weekend?" They might say, "Well, I have to go to work in the morning." I say some version of "No problem, I don't have to speak until tomorrow at 9:00 a.m. I'll drive you to work, OK?" At that point, they might say, "Well, I'll need to get home after work." Again, no problem, I say. "I'll pick you up."

When we've gotten to this point, we've addressed most of the needs, but there are usually some fears such as, "How do I know I can trust you, Dr. Monastra?" to which I say, "I'm a licensed psychologist, with a family, home, and clinic in New York. I can give you a copy of my driver's license and insurance card. Do you think I'd risk losing all of that by stealing your car, especially in front of all these witnesses?" Again, more laughter, but the point was made.

By systematically addressing the foundation of *no*, you can typically get what you want, without getting into trouble.

Let's take a kid example—a pretty serious one. A 17-year-old I'll call Michael and his father got into an argument over his request to go out with his friends. On a Friday night, Michael had asked and was permitted to go with his friends to a football game and then out for some food. He got home within the agreed-on curfew window. The next day, Michael asked his father if he could go out on Saturday night. His father said, "No, you went out last night. I want you to stay home."

Now instead of asking his father some version of "What's getting in the way, Dad?" Michael began to argue. "Why can't I go out tonight? You let me go out last night, and I didn't get into any trouble," he asserts. Unfortunately, that wasn't the issue, and they never found out Dad's real reason for telling Michael he had to stay home. Michael kept Whyning until his father became angry over his son's attitude and told him that he was grounded for the following weekend. This rapidly turned into a big blowup and even escalated to father and son wrestling on the floor before Mom broke it up.

I saw the boy and his parents on Monday. After reviewing the facts of life (i.e., wrestling with your father when he says no can land you in the hospital or an inpatient psychiatric facility) and evaluating medication issues with Michael and his parents, we applied a needs and fears analysis to their situation. Here's what came out.

Michael's father (after getting past the "Why does a kid need to go out on Friday and Saturday" roadblock) was able to recognize the following needs and fears. First, and most important, Michael's dad missed spending time with his son. Throughout his son's life, Michael and his father had spent time on the weekend together— sometimes fishing, sometimes hunting, sometimes going to a home improvement store then working on some building project, and sometimes just getting a burger together. As Michael grew older, and particularly after he turned 16, these times together had gotten pretty rare. His dad mostly needed some time with his son. He also wanted his son to help with a few chores on Saturday. There were no particular fears about his son "getting into trouble."

The discussion centered on how to take care of his dad's needs for some time with his son and getting Saturday chores done, while still allowing Michael to head out with his friends. Michael and his dad decided that Saturday mornings were "their time." They did some chores, typically spent some time outdoors, and never had a repeat of this problem.

Now you may be wondering if your child is old enough to learn how to ask what your need or fear is. The answer is this: If the child is old enough to Whyne, that child is old enough to learn how to ask "what." Even before children had the language skills to formulate the words *please* and *thank you*, you modeled it for them. You kept on reminding (and reinforcing) them to "say please, say thank you" until they got it. Just as you once modeled "please and thank you," when your child starts to whine or get mad hoping it will get her what she wants, you can have her practice saying, "What's getting in the way, Mom?" "What are you afraid of, Dad?" or "What do you need me to do so that you're OK if I . . . ?"

Now, fast-forward to later in life. Unless you teach this life lesson, that 7-year-old child who gets a payoff from crying, whining, stamping his feet, or storming out of the room will one day become the teenager who yells, swears at you, uses obscene language, and slams the door on the way out.

TIPS FOR TEACHING KIDS TO GET WHAT THEY WANT BY LEARNING OTHERS' NEEDS AND FEARS

The goal of this life lesson is to teach children how to overcome roadblocks and achieve their goals by discovering the needs and fears of others and then systematically taking care of these issues.

When I teach this class at my clinic, I begin by asking kids the following question: "What are kids supposed to do if they ask for something but their mom or dad says no?" Whether you are teaching your child at home or conducting a class at school, in your office, or at a clinic, I'd suggest that you start the conversation with your version of that question.

Then say something such as, "Today I want to show you a way to get what you want without having to beg, scream, whine, get mad, or cry. Are you ready? Here's the trick.

"When Mom or Dad says no to you, it means that they need something from you or are worried about something. If you can find out what it is, most of the time you'll be able to get what you want or something pretty close to it. Here's a story that can show you what I mean.

"A child wanted a video game. He asked Mom and Dad, 'Can we please go to the store and buy a new video game?' But they said no. Instead of saying, 'Why, why, why' or 'Please, please, please,' or throwing stuff down, or yelling 'I hate you' and running off, the child said, 'Mom . . . Dad, what is it? Are you afraid of something? Do you need me to do something to earn it?'

"Dad said, 'I'm worried that if I get you another video game, all you'll do is sit around and play inside. I want you getting exercise and joining a sports team.' Mom said, 'I don't like you playing violent games. I'm worried that you'll start fighting with your brother.'"

At this point stop and ask your child:

Did you hear any fears? There are three (child won't go outside, won't exercise, will become more violent).

Did you hear any needs? There is one (desire for the child to become involved in sports).

Continue with the lesson, saying, "So this is what the child in the story said: 'Mom, Dad, if I sign up for Little League baseball and play outside after school for at least 30 minutes a day, can we get a new game at the end of the week?'

"His parents said, 'That sounds pretty good, but we're still worried that you might start hitting your brother.'

"Their son said, 'Mom, Dad, if I hit my brother, then you can take the game away from me for a week!'

"His parents said OK."

You can summarize the story like this: "Now let's try to remember what the child did. First, he asked politely. Then, when his parents said no, he asked them _____ [pause and wait for the child or class to say what the parents were afraid of or needed]. When he found out what they were afraid of and needed, the child said _____ [pause and wait for the child/class to say what the child offered to do]."

If you don't want to use the video game example, you could talk about other situations when a parent might say no because his or her needs or fears are in the way, for example, asking to go to the mall with friends, asking to sleep over at a friend's house, or asking to see a particular movie.

In my clinic, the challenge that goes with this activity is for children in the class to come up with as many parental needs and fears as they can think of in 2 minutes for each situation. I'll allow parents to "scribe" and write down answers, but I want the students to come up with the reasons. The child with the highest number of reasons earns the prize for that night.

As a parent, something you might be wondering right now is, "Does all of this mean that my child should be able to get or do anything that she or he wants?" My answer is this: Your child will learn a lot about how to solve problems by finding out what's getting in the way of your saying yes to a request and brainstorming ways to take care of your needs and fears. But that doesn't mean anything goes. All parents have some version of what they believe is right or wrong. In some families, these beliefs are based on religious teachings. In other families, these beliefs are based on the laws of their country, which they have accepted as worthwhile principles to teach their children. In any case, it boils down to "certain actions or things are just not okay for my kid."

Let's see how that plays out in real life. Let's say that you are a parent who believes it is wrong to kill and you take this belief one step further: You think that because it is wrong to kill, it's not OK for your children to watch movies or television programs where killing is shown in great detail for entertainment. You might even think that it's not OK for your child to practice killing on video games for amusement. If that's the case, a need or fear isn't the issue. The request goes against your moral principles, and there is no debating when it comes to that. Your child needs to know that in your family, you have one Golden Rule: Mom and Dad will not give you permission to do something that they believe is morally wrong. Period!

After discussing how needs and fears work, challenge your child with an activity such as the Problem-Solving Worksheet at the end of this lesson.

Worksheet for Life Lesson 3: Getting What You Want Without Getting Into Trouble Problem-Solving Worksheet

Let's practice getting what you want when someone says no. What it usually takes is figuring out what the other person needs or fears. Once you figure that out, it's pretty easy to come up with some solutions. Let's practice one situation and then try to get you something that you want for real.

Here's the pretend situation. Let's say that it's 6:30 at night, and a show that you want to watch is coming on in 2 hours, at 8:30. You ask your mom and dad if you can stay up and watch, but they say no. So what can you do?

Well, you could yell, tell them they're not fair, that other kids can stay up a lot later than you do, and go on and on . . . but that's not likely to work.

OR

You could try to figure out what they need or fear. You could say, "Mom and Dad, can we talk about me watching the show tonight? What's making you say no? Is it something you need me to do? Is there something you're worried about?"

THINK FOR A MINUTE . . . BREATHE
What kind of fears could be getting in the way? What could your parents possibly need from you? Take a couple of minutes and fill in these lines:

Mom/Dad might be afraid that I'll _____.
Or maybe they're afraid that I'll _____.
Or maybe they need me to _____.
Or maybe they need _____.

Now that you have some ideas of why your parents might say no, let's come up with some ways that you could take care of the problem so they'll say yes.

Idea 1: I could _____.
Idea 2: I could _____.
Idea 3: I could _____.
Idea 4: I could _____.

Worksheet for Life Lesson 3: Getting What You Want Without Getting Into Trouble Problem-Solving Worksheet (*Continued*)

Now let's try the real thing. Think about something you want or would like to do but your parents have said no. Let's see if you can find out what your parents' needs or fears are and figure out some ways to take care of them so that you can get what you want.

Step 1: Write down what it is that you want or would like to be able to do.

_____

Step 2: Ask politely (say "please").

Step 3: Parents/grandparents/other caregivers say no.

Step 4: You ask: What's getting in the way? Are you worried about something? Do you need me to do something?

Do they need something? If so, what is it?

_____

_____

Are they afraid or worried about something? If so, what are they worried about?

_____

_____

Step 5: Now, talk with your parents and write down some ways that you could take care of their needs or fears and still get what you wanted.

Idea 1: _____

Idea 2: _____

Idea 3: _____

Once you have some ideas that can work, pick the ones that you and your parents like. Beats whining, doesn't it?

BEING CONFIDENT, PART I: MASTERING SOMETHING THAT MATTERS TO YOUR PEERS

Have you ever wondered why some people seem pretty brave and others are scared to try anything new? If you happen to have more than one child, you've probably seen this in your own family. One child is outgoing, has lots of friends, is involved in school activities, and has no problem volunteering to try something new. Another child will seem timid, introverted, and insecure and has had the same one friend since kindergarten. How does this happen?

There are a lot of theories about this. One line of thought is that some children are born with a tendency to be more of an "explorer" and wander away from their parents. Others are born with a tendency to stay close to the nest. Another perspective is that these tendencies are related to parent modeling, teaching, encouragement, and the role of peer acceptance. From what I've read, the predominant perspective among psychologists, pediatricians, and other child development specialists is that a combination of life experiences and genetics are relevant for understanding the foundation of confidence.

I remember being a little kid and my sister would have to supervise me pretty closely for the two of us to walk to school and get there on time. I'd notice all sorts of things during the walk. I'd want to explore vacant buildings, follow streams of ants, improve my pitching arm by throwing stones at poles, or count the number of cars that were a particular color, for example. I was simply more interested in anything other than getting to school on time. The grown-up version of me still has that explorer streak. The kid version of me wanted to check out everything *but* the way to school, and my sister took on the job of getting me there safely. The grown-up version of me is busy noticing billboard details, the scenery, or whatever catches my attention, while my wife makes sure I don't drive through the red lights so we get to our destination safely.

In contrast, the nonexplorer, clingy, "shy" kids will also have the tendency to hold on to their reserved approach throughout their lives. They are the children who shed those heart-melting tears when they head off to pre-K and are terrified to go onto the field during sports practices and games. During their later childhood and teenage years, these are the kids who stay at home, resist becoming involved in any activities, and may fail to blossom. Although a lot of these shy toddlers get over their hesitation after experiencing the fun at preschool or soccer, some will still need a lot of encouragement to get involved in activities, even as teens. As long as they eventually begin to get into the game of life and find some measure of success they, too, will come to realize that they feel better and more confident when they participate. When it comes to the sources of confidence, the process of attempting to master something that matters to people one's age is considered to be a biggie, but it's not the only source.

Attempts to define *confidence* typically emphasize the definition that confidence is "a feeling or belief that you can do something well or succeed at something" (*Merriam–Webster's Collegiate Dictionary*; http://www.merriam-webster.com). The simple translation is that confidence is the feeling of "I'm OK." It's that belief deep in our core that we've got as good of a chance as anyone to succeed in what we try. It's that belief that even if we don't succeed the first time, it's OK;

it will just take a little more practice. It's that belief that if someone laughs or makes fun of us when we don't succeed, it's OK; no one is perfect. Many theorists, like Dr. Abraham Maslow, consider confidence or self-esteem to be a basic human need. This leads to some obvious questions: Where does confidence come from? How does it develop? How do we "feed" this need?

WHERE DOES CONFIDENCE COME FROM?

One of the best presentations I've read about the sources of confidence was from Dr. Stanley Coopersmith. In his book *The Antecedents of Self-Esteem,* Dr. Coopersmith shared the perspective that self-esteem is derived from a number of beliefs that come from our life experiences, including the following:[1]

- the belief that I "look good" in the eyes of my parents,
- the belief that I am good at (or are getting better at) an activity or task that matters to people my age,
- the belief that I can face and succeed in situations that are anxiety provoking,
- the belief that I am liked by others, and
- the belief that I am living my life according to my moral code.

From this perspective, if you want a child's confidence to grow, you will need to help her develop each of these beliefs. In this lesson, we'll talk about ways to build confidence based on relationships with parents and peers and by mastering skills that matter to others. In the next lesson, we'll focus on building confidence by facing fears. Later in this book, we'll review ways to build confidence by living a life that matches a child's moral code.

---

[1] Coopersmith, S. (1981). *The antecedents of self-esteem* (2nd ed.). Palo Alto, CA: Consulting Psychologists Press.

TIPS FOR BUILDING CONFIDENCE AT HOME

The first step in promoting confidence starts at home. The question for you is pretty straightforward: Do you think that your child believes that he looks good in your eyes? If you doubt it, then you can start to build this belief by introducing a few simple routines in your home.

Point Out What Your Child Did Right Today

First, remember that if you have a child with attention-deficit/ hyperactivity disorder (ADHD), odds are he or she will get more criticism than compliments on a day-to-day basis. These children will hear parents' reminders—both patient or impatient—of all the things they've forgotten, all the things they failed to do, all the things they should have done better, and all the frustration that comes when they have to be reminded over and over again. They'll have similar experiences at school with their teachers. So by the time they get home, it's not uncommon for kids with ADHD to be a little on the edgy side. Which leads me to suggestion Number 1: Every day, make sure to take the time to tell your child something he or she really did right that day!

Spend at Least 15 Minutes Each Day
Hanging Out With Your Child

Second, because parents spend so much time correcting their child with ADHD, it's easy to get into the trap of grilling our children whenever we see them: "Do you have any homework? What do you mean you did it at school? Did you get in trouble today? Did you remember to make your bed (pick up your clothes, bring in the garbage cans, feed the dog, etc., etc., etc.)?" So the second suggestion is this: Set aside at least 15 minutes when you just "hang out" with your child.

Do you think you can be in a room with your child for 15 minutes each day and not ask a single question, give a single direction, teach her in any way, or criticize her for any of her actions during the day? It sounds easy but will likely be hard for you at first. Think of this as a time when you might play a game on a computer with your child (prepare to be soundly defeated). It may be a time when you read a book together and talk about what's going on in the book. It could be a time when you watch a TV show together and actually talk about what's happening. Maybe it's a time when you play a Minute-to-Win-It skill game (http://www.nbc.com/minute-to-win-it; or do a search for "Minute-to-Win-It Games"). Or you could play Truth or Dare with your child. If you've never played this, you'll be amazed what happens in this game. The deal is this: You take turns asking each other the question "Truth or Dare?" If the person says "Truth," he has to answer truthfully whatever question is posed. If the person says "Dare," he has to do whatever challenge you give him.

At the End of Each Day, Express Your Love for Your Child

The third suggestion has to do with the end of the day. It is simply this: Take a few moments at bedtime to express your love for your child. Use the last few moments of the day to let them know what they did that you appreciated or made you smile. The times you caught them doing something kind, or made you think about how special your child is to you. Everyone likes to hear about the good stuff they did. What better time than right before you go to sleep?

If you take on these challenges, you'll be amazed how hard it is, at first. But as you come to realize that you're spending much of your time with your child grilling them or directing them, you'll hopefully wake up to the reality that there is very little time that your child is getting the impression that they "look good" in your eyes. That is something worth fixing, because if they don't believe that you think they're awesome, in the end, it won't really matter if someone else does.

WHAT DO YOUR CHILD'S PEERS CARE ABOUT?

After you've started working on the "Do I look good in your eyes, Mom or Dad?" question, you're ready to take on the next step. Whether you're teaching this lesson at home or in a group setting, the lesson begins with a simple question to the child(ren), "What matters to kids your age?" It shouldn't surprise you to learn that the kids in my classes typically mention the things they *own* first.

Truth is, they are right when they tell me that the brand of sneakers they have, the kind of clothes they wear, the kind of game system they play, or the kind of cell phone they have matters to kids their age. If you happen to own the newest kind of cell phone or wear $200 sneakers, it will impress someone and increase your "likeability" among some groups of kids. And although most of us realize that what we own isn't the only thing that matters, it is one source of confidence. So when the kids in my class mention that other kids may like them a bit more because of what they own, I don't argue that point.

Instead, I rephrase the question slightly to "What kinds of activities or skills matter to kids your age?" As we brainstorm this one, I start to find out some pretty interesting things about my patients. As you get this conversation started, you can use the worksheet for Life Lesson 4 as an organizer. Don't be surprised if your child or others in your group list getting good at video games as one of the things that matter. At the time of this writing, a lot of children and teens are into Minecraft, which is a pretty fascinating building game that's sort of part LEGO® creativity and part mindless destruction. Another commonly mentioned activity in my life skills groups is being good at a sport. Playing a musical instrument in a school band seems to count, but simply knowing how to play a musical instrument does not, at least in the classes I've run.

One thing that struck me as I've talked with kids is how early in life doing well at school matters to a child. When teacher ratings change from giving "super" stickers and "smiley" faces to everyone

Worksheet for Life Lesson 4: The "Get Good at Something That Matters" Challenge

One way that you can begin to grow in confidence is by getting good at something that matters to people your age. So if you want to become a little more confident, the first thing that you need to figure out is, "What matters to kids my age?" Does anyone in your class care if you are good at a particular video game or fantasy card game? Do kids in your class look up to someone who has mastered the complexities of Minecraft? Even though playing these games is fun, unless being good at them really matters to other kids, your skill won't build your confidence. How about being good at playing basketball or some other sport? Or playing a musical instrument and being part of the school band? Do these abilities matter? If so, getting good at these kinds of activities would boost that sense of inner strength or confidence.

Because it's been a long time since your parents have been in school, they probably don't know what matters to kids your age. So take a few minutes and write down what you think. Think about the kids in your class who seem to be confident. What do they spend their time doing? Fill in this Top 5 list.

Top 5 List: What Activities/Skills Matter to Kids My Age

1. _____
2. _____
3. _____
4. _____
5. _____

OK, now that you've got the list, look it over. Decide which one of these activities you are going to start doing in the coming month. Write down the new challenge that you are going to take on:

This month, I'm going to work on getting good at _____
_____
_____
_____

who finishes a task to number or letter grades, kids notice where they rank in their class. It doesn't matter whether the system is A to F, 4 to 1, or 100 to 50; kids notice, and it hits home, even in children who are supposedly distracted and don't pay close attention to details.

As part of my evaluation of children and teens, I'll take the time to read their report cards from kindergarten on up. Just how quickly a kindergartner's enthusiasm can change to discouragement, withdrawal, and defeat came home to me courtesy of a seventh-grade girl I'll call Becky. As a kindergartner, Becky was beaming. The smile in her kindergarten school photo was contagious and somewhat surprising for a little girl who was having a hard time learning to read, write, and do math. Her teachers thought that she was motivated but needed a lot of redirection and just didn't seem to be catching on. By the time she hit third grade, the smile was gone. She said very little in class, and teachers were concerned that she was depressed. At home, she watched a lot of TV, ate way too much junk food, and gained a lot of weight.

Her parents brought her to my clinic when she was in seventh grade. We started her treatment for ADHD and her parents signed her up for my life skills class. When we got to this lesson in class, she and a lot of the other kids wrote down that doing well at school made a person look good in the eyes of other kids. As we discussed this, one of the kids said, "No one wants to hang out with a kid who's doing bad in school. It makes other kids think you're stupid too!" Becky burst into tears. She had been ashamed of her grades for years, and now she was getting the confirmation that she feared: No one would ever want to be her friend because she wasn't good at school.

Being part of that life skills class turned out to be one of the best things that ever happened to Becky. With the help of the other kids and her parents, she came to understand that other kinds of skills also mattered to kids her age, and she started doing the things she could do well. From time to time, I'll see Becky around town. She'll always greet me with a huge, "Yo, Dr. M!" and tell me about her latest adventures.

Her smile is back and even though she never got great at reading, writing, or math, she's turned into a pretty good chef.

I thought about Becky another time, more recently. I was talking with my son, Julian (who prefers being called Jay). Jay is a third-grader who is this amazingly loving boy with a smile that lights up pretty much any room he's ever been in. He's got a great memory, he's outgoing, and loves to share stories. He also has a great love of food and enjoys cooking with me and his mom. His career goal: to own The Monastra Family Italian Restaurant.

Now, because none of us is good at everything, Jay has his limitations, too. Math comes pretty hard for him. Writing is a challenge. And he's been working on overcoming a vision problem that made reading tricky. Even knowing this, it stunned me when one day, he came home from his day at school, then a second-grader, and broke down at homework time, sobbing and saying, "I'm stupid, I can't do anything right! My brother's better than me at everything! Nobody likes me! Why did God make me this way? I wish I was anybody but me."

I'm supposed to be a pretty decent dad and psychologist, with a lot of experience. But I was floored. After all, I'd just heard one of the saddest things anyone would ever want to hear their child say. But then inspiration hit, and I said, "Jay, I want to ask you a couple of questions. Who has the better memory, you or Diego [his brother]?" He says, "I do." I continue: "OK, who has the smile that everyone loves?" He says, "I do." I say, "OK, who is great at telling stories?" Again, he says "I am." I keep going: "Who loves to cook?" Again the answer is "I do!" The last question I ask is, "Who wants to own a restaurant when he grows up?" The answer: "I do!" So I said, "Hmmm, if God wanted to build a great restaurant owner, what would be better than to give him a great smile, a super memory, a gift for telling stories, and a love for food and cooking?" My son smiled the biggest smile ever, and said, "You're right, Dad!" and we plowed through the homework. The issue has never come up again.

As you talk with your child, or others in your support group, remember that helping them take on the challenge of getting good at something that matters is an important step. Just like all of the previous lessons, it's a challenge that you'll need to talk about on a week-to-week basis until the lesson sticks.

TIPS FOR TEACHING CONFIDENCE IN GROUPS

Getting good at something that matters to peers helps develop confidence. So when I offer this class at my clinic, the Challenge Game involves beginning to do a new task in front of other people. I'll often pick some type of puzzle board that the child attempts to solve at the front of the class. It could be a labyrinth type of game in which the child has 60 seconds to see how far she can get through the maze. It could be a pegboard game (Lafayette Pegboard) in which the child tries to place a group of small, grooved, metal pegs into slots. It could be a paper airplane game in which the child folds a sheet of paper into a plane and attempts to land it in on a target within 60 seconds. It doesn't matter what game you choose; the idea is the same. The child gets up in front of a group of peers and attempts a task. By doing so, he realizes that it's not the end of the world if he tries and at first does not succeed. This activity and lesson sets the stage for all of the other lessons, because in each of the coming lessons, the children will be trying to learn some "new skills" in front of their peers.

BEING CONFIDENT, PART 2: FACE YOUR FEARS

Everyone is afraid of something. It doesn't matter if it's the dark, the diving board at the pool, heights, elevators, spiders, being ignored, a nasty look from another person, a mean comment from someone, or doing something in front of other people (like playing a sport, going out on the dance floor, or giving a talk in front of the class). It's all the same. No matter what the source of our fear is, our body does the same thing. Our breathing gets shallow, we take in less oxygen, our heart rate increases, our digestive system shuts down, blood flow gets diverted from the brain to muscles, and we prepare to fight, flee, or freeze.

Sometimes, people have a misconception about kids with attention-deficit/hyperactivity disorder (ADHD). They mistakenly think these kids aren't be likely to have many fears because they are so distracted and forgetful. I guess the idea is that kids with ADHD wouldn't notice that they "should" be afraid. In fact, the opposite is the case. Children and teens with ADHD are 3 to 4 times more likely to be diagnosed with an anxiety disorder than kids without ADHD. The rate of children with ADHD and an anxiety disorder ranges from about 20% to 50%. Like the other problems children and teens with ADHD experience, anxiety will typically not go away by itself. It is important for you to consult with your child's physician and therapist to decide on the best strategies to help your child begin to build confidence by facing his or her fears. I hope the strategies I share with you in this lesson will be useful to you and the members of your child's clinical team.

Clinical researchers such as Dr. Joseph Wolpe, Dr. Thomas Stampfl, and Dr. Donald Levis spent decades learning about ways to help people overcome anxiety. Dr. Wolpe developed a type of treatment called *systematic desensitization*. Dr. Stampfl and Dr. Levis examined an approach they called *implosive therapy*. Both of these approaches are based on one simple truth: To overcome fear, you need to experience a sense of calmness in the situation that you fear. If you're afraid of snakes, you'd need to experience a sense of calmness in the presence of a snake.

Pretty simple, right? Hardly. People tend to flee or avoid situations that they fear, not head toward them. If you have ever tried to help a child overcome a fear, you know exactly what I mean. The child who is afraid to jump off the diving board isn't likely to come up to you and say, "Hey, Mom, let's go over to that terrifying diving board so that I can jump off and get braver!" The child who is terrified of trying a new food isn't likely to remind you at the grocery store to pick up those scary green beans to help her get braver.

You also know that talking rationally with your child doesn't help. If children are afraid of trying string beans, telling them it's OK, they'll be fine, and they won't choke isn't likely to help. If they are afraid of trying out for a team, telling them it's OK, they'll be fine, and no one will laugh at them isn't likely to work. Although parent reassurance that a situation is safe can be helpful, children have to do something that defies logic: They need to move toward that which they fear.

NAVIGATING THE BRAVE PLACE AND THE SCARED PLACE

To explain the idea of getting confident through facing fears, it can help to imagine that in the land of our fears, we have a Brave Place and a Scared Place. In both these places, we find relief. However, traveling to one of these places builds confidence; the other leads to ongoing anxiety and fear.

When you experience a moment of anxiety or fear, you have two choices: Face the fear, go through it, and journey to the Brave Place or flee from the fear (or remain frozen) in the Scared Place. If you choose to journey to the Brave Place, you'll experience anxiety for a brief period, but after you survive what you feared, your body calms, you feel at peace, and your confidence grows. You take the step forward, do whatever it was that frightened you, and find peace in the Brave Place.

The Scared Place is where you are (and what you feel) before you take on whatever it is you are afraid of. If you're afraid of trying something new, the Scared Place is the land where you don't make that step forward and take on the new task. You turn from what you fear, walk away, and make some excuse such as, "Learning to ski is boring." You may feel a sense of calm as you get away from the Scared Place, but there's no gain in confidence. Deep inside, you know it, too.

Like the fear experts learned, *where* the person feels that state of calmness makes all the difference in the world when it comes to overcoming fear. If I run away from (or avoid) what I fear and feel calm there, then I am learning to feel calm in the Scared Place. So I'll continue to feel scared. On the other hand, if I move toward what I fear and experience calmness there, then I am learning to feel calm in the Brave Place. If I do that, I'll begin to feel brave and more confident.

The two approaches for overcoming fear that I mentioned (desensitization and implosive therapy) are a little different. Desensitization is a strategy that helps a person overcome fear by breaking it down into small steps and taking one little bite out of anxiety at a time. The child is first taught a way to get into a calm state by learning how to control her breathing (we talked about this in Lesson 2). Next, the child who fears string beans may be asked to look at a picture of a string bean until she is able to have that calm, brave feeling while looking at the picture. After she mastered that step, she might work on keeping that brave feeling while holding a green bean, and then licking a green bean, and then taking a little nibble of a green bean, and so on. The idea is to learn to feel that calm sensation when moving toward what we fear, rather than fleeing. One mother once told me that she had to put a new food on her child's plate about 10 times before he would even taste it.

Implosive therapy moves more quickly. Instead of overcoming fear a little bit at a time, this is more of an "all-in" approach. With the presence of a parent, therapist, or other helper, the child is encouraged to go to the Brave Place until the sense of calmness develops. In implosive therapy, the child who is getting over a fear of a swimming pool might be encouraged to jump into the pool, landing in his mom's or dad's arms. Some kids will do this, and the results are instantaneous. Calmness and braveness develop pretty quickly, and within a few tries, the *parent* may begin to worry that their child will jump into any pool, at any depth.

If the parents were using desensitization to help their child get over a fear of the swimming pool, they might have their child first sit on the side of the pool, then gently move his hand or toes in the water, then sit on the side of the pool with his legs in the water, then walk to the ladder or steps leading into the water and let the water go up to his ankles, and then finally hold his parent's hand and walk about in the water. Again, the goal is to get that calm feeling in the Brave rather than the Scared Place. Once again, your child's physician and therapist can help guide you regarding which approach would be a good fit for your child.

Whatever approach you and your child prefer, the goal of this lesson is to begin to help your child realize three important truths:

1. Everyone is afraid of something.
2. Avoiding what you fear leads to more anxiety.
3. Facing what you fear builds confidence.

So let's get started. First, give your child (or your class) the following Bravery List worksheet. The list is not meant to be all-inclusive, but just a starting point. The child is to complete the list with a parent's help because most of us tend to draw a blank when it comes to remembering our fears.

Worksheet for Life Lesson 5: Bravery List

Everyone, and I mean everyone, is afraid from time to time. But the truth is that if you can somehow get yourself to step forward and do what you are afraid of, you will grow in confidence. If you don't, then you'll stay scared. One way to gain confidence is to take on some of your fears. Start by writing down the first thing that comes to mind in each of the following situations:

When I'm at home, I feel scared or worried when

1. _____
2. _____

When I'm at school, I feel scared or worried when

1. _____
2. _____

When I'm at the playground or park, I feel scared or worried when

1. _____
2. _____

(continued)

Worksheet for Life Lesson 5: Bravery List (*Continued*)

When I'm playing sports, I feel scared or worried when

1. _____

2. _____

When I'm performing in front of others (like giving an oral presentation, playing music, doing gymnastics, dancing, or acting in a play), I feel scared or worried when

1. _____

2. _____

When I go to a store or a restaurant with my parents, I feel scared or worried when

1. _____

2. _____

IT DOESN'T HAVE TO BE HERO STUFF

Now that we have a list to work from, ask your child to select at least one fear each day to work on. This doesn't have to be hero stuff. It really is as simple as eating that green bean you're terrified of; making eye contact and saying hi to someone instead of looking away; walking onto a neighborhood basketball court and asking, "You guys need one more player?"; wearing your favorite shirt to school, even though you're not sure it's "cool"; actually singing during chorus; or trying out for a team, play, or band, even if you don't think you're the greatest. It's such a great feeling to experience the calm that comes from being in the Brave Place.

Celebrate even the smallest successes with your child. Ask your child, how did it feel to try _____? Are you glad you did it? What do you think trying _____ will allow you to do in the future? The idea here is to help your child make the connection that each feat, no matter how small, will lead them to experience calm in the Brave Place, which will help them grow in confidence.

In every life skills class that I teach, I am always heartened to see kids working together to help each other face their fears. Boys who are pretty comfortable with their athletic skills will help another kid in the class join their team and work with their buddy to get better. Girls in the class who are active on swim teams, gymnastics teams, Girl Scouts, a 4-H club, or other activities will arrange to introduce their friend from class to their team or activity. One thing that is helpful for a child or teen is to learn that at least one child in the class is afraid of something that they are not. Just the simple realization that "I've mastered a fear that others haven't" can boost a child's confidence. Because when children think about it, they begin to remember the good feeling that came from a time that they journeyed from the Scared Place to the Brave Place.

Reading with your children about the lives of men and women who faced their fears and accomplished amazing feats can also be helpful. Many very famous people typically faced and overcame fear after fear after fear on their way to success. I think of a very small boy named Bruce Lee who, despite his size, faced his fears of competing against much bigger and stronger men and became the most famous martial artist of his day. Or a boy named George Herman "Babe" Ruth who was placed in a home for "bad" boys by his parents and overcame the anxiety of being separated from them to become arguably the most famous baseball player of all time. As you and your child read about the lives of famous people and how they faced and overcame fear, I hope your child will be encouraged too.

Once your child begins to take on this challenge, he or she will quickly learn that taking on fears can be fun, once you have a little success. It doesn't matter whether your child is one who takes on fear "a bite at a time" or pinches his or her nose and swallows the whole fear all at once. The important thing is to get started.

TIPS FOR TEACHING KIDS TO OVERCOME THEIR FEARS

For a challenge activity in a group setting, ask the kids to take out a piece of paper and write down the names of each of the other kids in the class. Next to each name, have them to take a guess at one thing that they think that child is afraid of. Then have everyone look at their Bravery List. Every time another child correctly guesses one of the fears on their list, the other child scores a point. This back-and-forth exchange between kids reaffirms the notion that everyone is afraid of something and also helps kids realize that they have in fact overcome a number of fears. In the end, the child with the most correct answers wins the prize for the class (typically cash, a check, or gift certificate worth about $15). In the event of a tie score, the bonus question is to guess what they think makes me anxious.

If you are teaching this lesson at home, I like playing variations of Truth or Dare, where you and your child take turns asking, "Truth or dare?" If the person says "Truth," then she has to answer the question truthfully. If she says "Dare," then she has to do whatever she is asked to do. It's a lot of fun and often very helpful because parents can share some of the things that they feared and overcame over the years. This also gives everyone in the family the opportunity to take a "dare" and do something that will probably produce some anxiety but lead to that Brave Place where calmness and confidence grow.

The other thing that I ask parents and children to do at home is for everyone in the family to begin doing one thing that makes them anxious every day. For example, in my family, one of my sons gets pretty uptight about eating new foods. But to be honest, everyone else in the family gets a "yucky" feeling over at least one type of food. For me, it's mushy foods like oatmeal. So to help him face this fear, he got to pick one new food for everyone in the family to try, and he needed to eat the one we picked. It was much more fun than we thought it would be.

FINDING OUT WHAT OTHERS LIKE TO TALK ABOUT

One of the hardest parts of growing up with attention-deficit/ hyperactivity disorder (ADHD) has to do with making and keeping friends. When a child is 3 or 4 years old, it doesn't matter if she doesn't talk and pretty much ignores other kids. As long as she doesn't get mad and bite, kick, or hit someone, the playground works out pretty well. Play dates for these kids aren't so much for the kids themselves as they are for the parents, who are often seeking out any and all opportunities for adult conversation.

A good play date often translates to a couple of kids hanging out in the same general area and finding a way to not hurt their play date buddy as they climb all over each other getting to the Thomas the Train table. The better their little friend's stuff, the better the play date. The fact that no words were ever exchanged during the 2 hours plays no role in the success of the play date. The mere act of sharing toys is a rite of passage for your child, providing a glimpse of what the future holds as she transforms from "untamed and primitive" to a socialized being.

This kind of social networking continues during kindergarten. Parents will try to arrange play dates for kids, and the routine is pretty much the same. A couple of kids play in a sandbox, hang out at the community pool or "climber," with their parents keeping a watchful eye as they socialize with other parents in the shade. The children aren't really expected to have conversations. Again, all they need to be able to do is to share toys, take turns, and run around.

All of this starts to change during the primary grades. Instead of just running around in circles on the playground during recess, kids will start to pair off or become part of a group that will spend time together talking about what's funny or interesting to the group. As this starts to take place, some kids struggle to fit in. They have difficulty knowing what to talk about. Even when they do have an idea, they don't know how to introduce the topic for discussion. As a result, they end up saying nothing or saying silly, ridiculous things. Pretty soon, other children will start to ignore them, and they begin to realize that they don't have any friends. Invitations to birthday parties stop coming. Invitations for play dates don't happen anymore. And, gradually, an important source of confidence begins to erode because your child starts to believe that no one wants to be his or her friend.

When I first started treating children and teens with ADHD, I noticed their difficulties having conversations pretty quickly. I'd ask these kids a question, and they would seem like they hadn't heard me, or if they did show some sign of registering what I'd asked, all they could come up with was some version of "mmm hmm" in response. By the time these "quiet" kids with ADHD got to my office as a middle school student, they'd simply sit in the room as their parents spoke and say pretty much nothing. Because these children were so quiet, parents and teachers would wonder if they were depressed, and a fairly high percentage of them would have been diagnosed with some type of mood disorder or bipolar disorder (particularly if they seemed sullen or became violent over "little stuff"). Before they ever got to my clinic, many of these children had been treated with antidepressant or mood-stabilizing medications that just made them worse.

The problem isn't that children with ADHD can't have a mood disorder. As with anxiety, kids with ADHD are 2 to 3 times more likely to develop a mood disorder that will need to be treated. However, from my perspective, the more likely problem for children with ADHD who are not hyperactive or overly talkative is that their ADHD will go undiagnosed or misdiagnosed as depression. That can lead to prolonged periods of discouragement for children with ADHD and confusion among parents about how to best help their child.

When I sat with these kids, I had a very different kind of feeling. These boys and girls weren't really depressed as much as they were "locked up." They seemed to have great difficulty following a conversation, much less coming up with something to say. Outside of maybe being able to talk about something they liked a lot, they really didn't participate in conversation.

Another group of kids had a lot to say. The problem is that they went on and on and on, and it didn't matter whether the person they were talking to had any interest in the topic. These are the kids that you say "hi" to and they immediately launch into the details of whatever TV show, movie, video game, or toy has caught their interest. Right now, it's something like Ninjago or Marvel Superheroes. Who knows what the new big thing will be when you are reading this book.

I remember an 8-year-old patient of mine, whom I'll call Jimmy. This boy was really into *Star Wars*. One day while sitting with him and his parents during a session, I asked him, "What did you do this weekend?" His parent answered first, telling me he had watched *Star Wars*. Naturally, I asked, "Tell me about it." So my patient began: "Well, doc, I love eating sour candies, and I couldn't believe it, but my mom and dad said I could have some. It was the biggest bag of those candies I ever had. I like eating the yellow ones first. My bag didn't have too many, but when I started eating them, they were good.

Skittles are pretty good but not so sour. My parents think that candy isn't good for me, but sometimes they let me have some. I really like Fruit Loops in the morning but I don't get that much." At that point, Jimmy's parents reminded him that he was going to tell me about *Star Wars*.

Jimmy started again, "I really liked it . . . it was so cool. The seats in the movie theater go back all the way. It's soooo comfy. I brought some of my *Star Wars* guys to the movie. I have Yoda and Luke Skywalker in his X-Wing Fighter and I really want to get the Emperor." Once again, Jimmy's parents reminded him to get back to the movie. Jimmy tried again: "It's really dark in the movies. Then the music starts, and there are a bunch of stars all over. And there are some words and the *Star Destroyer* is shooting at the Rebel Alliance and they're trying to save Princess Leia. . . ." And my little patient proceeded to give me the second-by-second description of the beginning of a *Star Wars* film.

His parents politely tried to redirect him once more, but that wasn't happening. Little Jimmy continued with incredible detail, hardly pausing for a breath as he described the actions of Han Solo, Luke Skywalker, Yoda, Darth Vader, and the rest of the heroes and villains of *Star Wars*. When his parents finally roped in his enthusiasm and got him to slow down so that we could discuss the "important stuff," Jimmy did stop. But then he didn't have much else to say, except periodically trying to get us back into a conversation about *Star Wars*.

WHY MAKING CONVERSATION IS HARD FOR PEOPLE WITH ADHD

At first, I really didn't get it. I mean, why would it be so hard for a child with ADHD to have a simple conversation? Then I and other clinical researchers began to look at the neurology and neurophysiology of ADHD. Our first job was to figure out what parts of the brain seemed to be involved in attention and behavioral control, because kids with ADHD were having lots of problems with those skills. We found that the frontal lobes of the brain and a region called the Rolandic cortex (which is located in the middle of the top part of the brain) seemed to be acting differently in children with ADHD compared with other children. These differences could be found on various kinds of brain scans, including electroencephalographs (EEGs), which are devices that measure the electrical activity in different parts of the brain.

When we looked at the EEGs of children and teenagers and began to track what was going on, we found that children with ADHD seemed to have different types of activity patterns in the frontal lobes and the Rolandic cortex than kids who did not have ADHD. We learned that the brain was like a five-speed engine. When it is working in first gear (producing activity called *delta* waves at about 0.5–3.0 Hz), a person is asleep. When it is producing brain waves in second gear (*theta* waves, about 4–8 Hz), the person may be awake, but if so, she is not aware. If she is reading, she will look at the words but then not be aware of what she just read. If someone is reading to her, she will not be aware of what the other person has said. If a child in this gear is in a classroom, he has no idea what the teacher has said. If his mom and dad are talking to him, he could look right at them and still have no clue what point they are trying to make. If he is asked to do something simple, like writing three sentences that include a certain spelling word, the child will go blank and not be able to come up with much. These are the inattentive moments that are among the most common symptoms of ADHD.

When the brain is working at faster speeds, an individual begins to be aware of what is going on around her. In third gear, the brain is producing what are called *alpha* waves (pulsing at about 9–11 Hz). At these speeds, the brain seems to be awake and aware, but the memory

99

and information recall centers of the brain are not fully engaged. We can focus on a flickering candle or our breathing and meditate, but memory and information recall centers of the brain are not firing. We can watch a television program in third gear and enjoy it but not remember many of the details (like the city where the program is taking place; the names of the characters; the day of the week, month, or year in which the action occurs; or even why the action is taking place). We're simply along for an entertainment ride.

In fourth and fifth gears (operating at speeds from 12–21 Hz), the brain is producing *beta* waves. At these speeds, the individual begins to notice details and is able to "think" about what is going on. If a student is reading, for example, he might notice a detail that would make him say, "Hmm, this might be on the test." If he is listening to a lecture, he might realize that the teacher seems to be taking extra time to go over a particular topic and say to himself, "Hmm, I'd better jot this down." If he is working on writing a paper, the frontal lobe, which does the task of gathering information from memory, is now in gear, and he would be able to recall important information, organize and plan how to start the paper, and begin to write down ideas.

When we compared the brain activity patterns of children and teens with ADHD and those without ADHD, we found that the majority of kids with ADHD showed underactivity or *hypoarousal* in the frontal lobes and the Rolandic cortex. Instead of speeding up, their brains seemed to stay stuck in second gear. When we calculated how much electrical activity was occurring in second gear (theta waves) and compared it with how much was occurring in fourth and fifth gears (beta waves), we found that this ratio (which we called the *theta/ beta ratio*) was much higher in patients with ADHD. These were not kids who were inattentive because they were thinking about lots of other things. These were kids who simply were not thinking or noticing much of anything because the parts of their brain that do that job weren't getting into the game. When they sat in my office and couldn't answer a question, it was because the frontal lobes of their brains were not activating enough to help them hear the question, understand its meaning, retrieve information that was needed to answer it, and then organize their ideas well enough to be able to say something.

Although most children with ADHD struggle to have conversations because the regions of the brain involved with attention and working memory are not activating, not all children with ADHD have this particular problem. Other children have excessively active frontal lobes. During quantitative EEG (QEEG) evaluation, we find that these children and teens have *hyperaroused* brains. They produce atypically low theta/beta ratios compared with kids who don't have ADHD. Instead of getting stuck in second gear (producing too much theta activity), their brains seem to get stuck in fifth gear (producing too much beta activity). Like my patient Jimmy, their brains jump from one thing to the next, to the next, to the next. They have a hard time having conversations not because they can't think of anything to say but because too much comes to mind, and their brains aren't particularly good at getting them to slow down, focus on one thing at a time, and stay on topic.

If you know a child with ADHD, whether it's your son or daughter, someone in your child's class, a kid on your sports team, a member of your Girl Scout troop, a next-door neighbor, or someone you teach or treat as a mental health counselor, you've seen one of these types of kids, or perhaps both. The big question is, how do we help them have the kinds of conversations that are so important in making and keeping friends?

TRAINING THE BRAIN TO STAY ON TOPIC

Moms and dads start encouraging the frontal lobe to develop pretty early in life. We first help our children have names for the things and people around them, and then teach them "action" words like *up, up, up, up, up* (to get picked up), *bubah* (to get a bottle), *Ma* (for mom to come), and *Da* (for dad to come). When they want something and know the word, the frontal lobe has to help them retrieve that information from memory, form words, and get them out. If they don't know a word, they'll simply cry.

Once our kids learn a basic vocabulary, we start helping them learn to develop categories for words. We teach them foods, colors, shapes, body parts, and so on. We teach them the letters of the alphabet and what the letters say. After endless hours of "A says ahh, B says buhh" and they have that knowledge in their memory centers, we can begin to play different kinds of games. These are activities in which we ask our child to say words in specific categories. Games that we would play include Grandma's Attic and lots of variations of Scattergories-type games.

Word and Category Games

In Grandma's Attic, the challenge is to come up with a different word for each letter of the alphabet and remember the all the words used. You begin with the letter A and the child will say, "In my Grandma's attic, I found an apple." The next person (could be a parent or another child) will continue by saying, "In my Grandma's attic, I found an apple and a baseball bat." The next person will say, "In my Grandma's attic, I found an apple, a baseball bat, and a cup." Your child and anyone else playing takes turns, remembering what the previous items were and then coming up with an item that begins with the next letter of the alphabet. There are different versions of this game, but my favorite has to do with stopping periodically to ask for a description of the object they mentioned (e.g., "What color is your baseball hat?" or "Tell me about the bear").

In the numerous variations of Scattergories-type games, the child is given a letter of the alphabet and has to say or write as many words as she can think of that are in a specific category in a brief period of time. When I test a child, I'll often use the category of "foods and drinks" because everyone knows a pretty large number of foods or drinks (any kind of food or drink is OK for this list, even candies, snack foods, sweet drinks). So I'll record the EEG of students as they are writing a list of foods and drinks beginning with the letter M or P or S (but not X, Y, or Z—not too many foods begin with those letters). You could ask a child to list the names of people, places, television shows, movies, or anything else you'd like, as long as you pick a specific letter of the alphabet to serve as the focus of the search. You could also simply ask the child to name as many words that begin with a specific letter (regardless of category).

If these games are too hard for your child, you might begin to work on rapidly naming colors, shapes, or objects. Take a sheet of paper, cut out some different-colored squares, and tape them in rows. The child needs to point to the square and rapidly name the color of the square. Or you can cut out pictures, arrange them in rows, and have the child name them as quickly as possible.

What's happening in these games is that the child's frontal lobes and the language and memory centers of the brain are teaming up to produce language that is "on topic." This is a biggie for all of us. If the regions of the brain are not developing and are not working as intensely as they should, having conversations that are on topic will be a real challenge. For this reason, spending time playing word games is an important part of the day not just for toddlers learning to speak but also for children and teens who need to get good at introducing, recognizing, and speaking about specific topics when they are with other kids.

Why Some Activities Don't Get the Brain in Gear as Well as Others

So let's take a minute and think about how much time your child or the children you teach or treat are practicing these kinds of skills. Sometimes families will try to have dinner conversations but find that the kids can't come up with anything to say. Sometimes families will try to play some kind of word game but find that their kids are quickly bored and would rather play video games or other electronic recreational activities (go onto any of the numerous interactive web-based games, check Facebook, surf the Internet, etc.).

Although each of these activities can be fun, stimulating, and interesting, something important is missing: There is no conversation going on. More important, when researchers examine the activity of the frontal lobes (which are involved in helping us organize our conversations) while we are engaged in these kinds of activities, these regions do not become more active. Instead, they seem to be disconnecting and going "offline." Although you probably don't have access to brain imaging equipment, I do. Let me share with you what I showed my children.

My sons Julian and Diego, like many kids, enjoy exploring the world of electronic games. They also happen to have access to all sorts of my high-tech, brain-measuring EEG equipment and have a dad who has been telling them for years that television and video games are like a brain binkie. They bring pleasure for sure, but they don't ask the frontal lobe to work.

My boys wanted to check this out for themselves. So they asked me if they could come into my clinic and see what was happening when they played their favorite video games, watched one of their favorite DVDs, viewed a favorite television show, read a book (and answered questions about it), played a working memory game (like writing down words that began with a specific letter and were in a specific category), completed some math problems, built something with LEGO® blocks, or went online and played some attention-training games on Lumosity (http://www.lumosity.com) or CogMed (http://www.cogmed.com), while I recorded the "pulse of the brain." They were surprised at the results, but I wasn't. Here's what they found out.

When they were playing video games or watching television or their favorite DVD, the frontal lobes of the brain simply checked out. Their theta/beta ratios indicated that their frontal lobes were "resting" (producing theta waves) 6 to 8 times more than they were producing beta waves. Kids their age without ADHD typically produce a ratio of about 3 to 1 when they are doing any type of activity that stimulates the frontal lobes.

On the other hand, when my children began to read a book, do math problems, or play a working memory game or attention-training game, their theta/beta ratio indicated about three resting periods for every attentive "brain-working period" (a 3:1 ratio), which is what the score should have been. Needless to say, their teachers were quite happy to see graphs that indicated reading, writing, and math woke up the frontal lobes. My little guys understood, even though they weren't as happy with the results as their teachers were.

So when you think about how much time your child is sitting watching a screen and pushing buttons to make little pixels move from place to place, building imaginary structures, smashing and hitting whatever comes their way, or blowing up other pixels, realize one thing: The part of the brain that needs to be developing for your child to be able to have conversations is just sitting on the sidelines. No one who plays Call of Duty pauses the screen, checks out the situation, determines how much ammo or "life" they have left, or how much farther they need to go before they finish the mission. They don't have to say anything to anyone. The game just calls us to push and click over and over and over again.

It doesn't matter how much life you have left in a video game, because you usually have endless lives; the frontal lobe doesn't need to pay attention to that. You don't have to worry about how much ammo you have because you either have endless ammo or endless lives, so who cares? Even if you run out of ammo, life force, or whatever, the game pauses briefly and then takes you right back to where you left off. The part of the brain that could be spending time developing the kinds of working memory skills needed for conversation is just idling while the visual-motor region of the brain is having a party.

Interaction Is Key

Here's my simple suggestion. Just like any other skill that you'd like your child to develop, working on the foundations of conversation is helpful. Whether you're reading together and talking about what you've read, playing a word game, doing some type of computerized attention training game, or doing one of the activities that we do in our life skills classes, spending a minimum of 20 minutes or so every day exercising the frontal lobes through some kind of activity that gives it a workout is a good idea for strengthening your child's ability to engage in conversations.

Although there are many ways you could begin to improve your child's conversation skills, reducing the amount of time spent in front of screens that don't require interaction and increasing the amount of time involved in conversation is a good place to start. When you begin to make that shift, you'll realize pretty quickly that your child has no idea what to talk about. In this lesson, we'll begin by teaching ways to figure out what other kids are interested in, discovering how to enter and sustain conversations, and then developing a network of kids with whom they do things. It all starts with learning what's important to others, because one of the essential truths about conversations is that people like to talk about their interests and experiences.

TIPS FOR TEACHING KIDS TO DISCOVER OTHERS' INTERESTS AND MAKE FRIENDS

If you want to help children begin to have the kinds of conversations that build friendships, it's important to help them discover what other kids like to talk about. Even though you can work on many of the other lessons in this book with one child, the next three lessons really require more than a single child. Usually, there are no shortages of kids in a school who aren't great at having conversations. You might have some friends who have children who could benefit from working together on conversational skills. The same is true at many recreational settings, like the YMCA. Speech therapists and mental health providers who work with children with ADHD and social (pragmatic) language disorders are also likely to be helping children who could benefit from such a life skills class.

Whether you do this on your own, with some friends, or with the help of a therapist at school or in your community, the first step in getting good at conversations is to learn what topics interest other kids. The problem is, most kids with ADHD aren't really great at figuring that out. They might manage a "Hey" or "What's up?" when they see someone they know. But after that, the conversation goes nowhere.

In my life skills class I first have the students experience what it's like to try to have a conversation without any clue about what the other kids like and then compare that with what it's like to have a conversation when you do have an idea about what others like. First, I'll have two kids walk up to two other kids in the class. I might have the other kids munching on some pizza at a table. The kids are asked to walk up, say some version of "Hi" or "What's up," and then see what happens.

Usually, what happens is that after the kids say "What's up," there's not much of an answer. There's just a shrug, followed by a deadly pause. No one has any idea what to say. Someone might start by asking a question such as, "Did you have any tests today?" or "Who do you have for your math teacher?" but again, it dies off pretty quickly.

You know how that feels, too. Picture yourself at a church picnic, a barbeque, or some other social gathering where you don't know many people. Or you see a neighbor you don't get together with often. You might say some version of hello, but face it, one of the most awkward moments that any of us can have is to sit next to someone and have no idea what to talk about. Oh sure, we can ask lame questions like, "How's it going?" or "What's new?" The problem with these questions is this: Our brains do not store information in a "how's it going, what's up, or what's new" category. If someone asks us, "What's up?" we might ask our frontal lobes to grab some information for us from the "what's up" storage area of our brain. But the odds are, our frontal lobes will come up empty.

Kids with ADHD have even more difficulty with this because the part of their brain that needs to wake up so that they can think about stuff to talk about doesn't activate as much as other kids' brains do. So when someone asks them, "How's it going?" or "What's up?" absolutely nothing comes to mind. I'll have kids in my class walk around and randomly ask each other "What's up?" and "How's it going?" to see what they get. I'll do the same thing. Usually, none of us will find someone who will come up with an interesting response. So if you're going to have conversations that don't bore you to death, you need to have an idea about what both you and others like to talk about.

After we pretty much come to the conclusion that saying "What's up?" or "How's it going?" leads nowhere, I'll give the students the following handout, which prompts them to list their interests and favorite activities. After each child has finished the list of his or her own likes, I challenge each one to take a turn standing in front of the group and say his or her name—nothing more. The other kids use their detective skills to guess what the kid in front of the class likes.

Worksheet 1 for Life Lesson 6: Discovering Your Own and Others' Interests

I like _____

I like _____

I like _____

I like to _____

I like to _____

I like to _____

Now use your detective skills to guess what other kids like. Write down your guesses here.

I think that _____ likes (to) _____

I think that _____ likes (to) _____

I think that _____ likes (to) _____

I think that _____ likes (to) _____

I think that _____ likes (to) _____

I think that _____ likes (to) _____

I think that _____ likes (to) _____

I think that _____ likes (to) _____

I think that _____ likes (to) _____

I think that _____ likes (to) _____

After everyone has taken a turn standing up, letting other kids guess what they like or like to do, then writing down their guesses, we play a game in which we see how good they are at guessing the interests of others. Each child will stand up again, and the other kids take turns calling out their guesses. Every time they correctly guess what the other student has written down on his or her list of likes, they get a point. I'll ask the children what helped them get it right. Sometimes it's about how the other student dressed. Sometimes a child might remember something that another child said during a previous class. Sometimes the child will guess based on what kids in their classroom talk about. I'll also pair the kids so that they can have some brief conversations with others who like the same type of things. That way, they can feel the difference in what a conversation is like when you know others' interests. In the end, the child who has guessed the most correct answers wins a prize. At my clinic, we usually give a monetary prize or a gift certificate valued between $10 and $15.

The main goal of these activities is to help your child develop a group of friends. If you are facilitating a support group, you might (with permission) obtain each child and parent's name and contact information and distribute it to the whole group as a way to encourage the kids to contact each other during the week.

Even with full contact information, most kids probably won't make an attempt to contact each other. To help your child practice, consider providing an incentive. You might require your child to make contact with another participant before they can use any electronic device. Or you might offer an opportunity to earn some other kind of fun experience. If you think it would be helpful, have your child use the Phone a Friend scorecard after each call to keep track of what they learned. If you want to encourage more family conversations, try the "How Well Do You Know Your Family?" worksheet too.

Worksheet for Life Lesson 6: Phone a Friend Scorecard

When is the last time you actually called a friend on the phone instead of texting, messaging, or commenting on their Facebook status or Instagram? Has it been a while? Those ways of connecting are OK for some things. They're fast, to the point, and let you get back to having fun on the Internet as quickly as possible.

Unfortunately, those kinds of quick communication bursts don't really prepare you for the kinds of conversations that lead to friendships beyond the surface. Plus, people can misunderstand each other pretty easily when they are only typing words and hashtags. To build strong, supportive friendships, you need plenty of extended conversations, in real time. Here are some tips for making your phone calls:

- Use a land line phone if you can find one, or another "dumb phone" that won't tempt you with all its other distractions.
- If you use a smartphone, tablet, or a computer for a video chat, stay off of any games or apps you might be tempted to use—at least until after your chat is over.
- Before you call, write down three stories you heard about, saw on TV, or found on the Internet that you thought were kind of interesting.
- Take a look at the sheet where you wrote down what you like and what other kids in your class like to do. You might start your conversations by asking the other kid if they did one of the things they liked today. Or you could pick one of the stories that you jotted down and start off the conversation with that.
- When the other person is talking, tell them about your reaction to what they are saying. Or you could ask them a question to get them talking more about what they did. Because the other kid can't see your face, those kinds of comments are the only way they'll get the idea that you are interested in them.

Here's the scorecard for you, to help you keep track of what you've learned.

(continued)

Worksheet for Life Lesson 6: Phone a Friend Scorecard (Continued)

My name: _____ Today is _____

I called _____

Here's what we talked about:

Good stuff that happened to them:

1. _____

2. _____

Lousy stuff that happened to them:

1. _____

2. _____

Good stuff that happened to me:

1. _____

2. _____

Lousy stuff that happened to me:

1. _____

2. _____

Stories I heard about from school, TV, or the Internet.

1. _____

2. _____

3. _____

(continued)

Worksheet for Life Lesson 6: Phone a Friend Scorecard
(*Continued*)

When we will talk next time or what we planned to do together: _____

_____

_____

_____

_____

Worksheet for Life Lesson 6: How Well Do You
Know Your Family?

A lot of the time, you might only talk to your parents about the lousy stuff in your life. They'll ask you questions such as, "Did you bring home your homework?" "Did you get your homework done?" "Do you have any tests?" "Did you get in trouble in school?" and "Did you make your bed?" They'll tell you to stop teasing your brother or don't bug your sister, leave their stuff alone, turn off the TV, get off the computer, or stop checking your Facebook messages and go to sleep. Somewhere in getting all our stuff done, we forget how it feels to just enjoy being a family.

To help you get that good feeling back (or make it stronger), play a guessing game with your parents. After you finish with them, your parents might want to do this with you and your brothers and sisters (if you have any). Take a few minutes and answer these questions. Then check your answers by talking with your parents. See how well you do.

1. What are your parents' favorite TV shows? _____

_____

2. What are your parents' favorite places to go? _____

_____

(continued)

113

Worksheet for Life Lesson 6: How Well Do You Know Your Family? (*Continued*)

3. What are your parents' favorite foods? _____

_____

4. What do your parents like to do for fun? _____

_____

5. What do your parents like to do with you? _____

_____

6. My parents would love it if I would _____

_____

Now you know some of the things that your parents like or like to do. Maybe instead of just talking about school, you can begin to start talking about what people like and like to do, which should make home time more fun.

SOMETIMES MAKING FACES CAN BE A GOOD IDEA

One of the lessons that kids are taught early in life is that making faces is a bad idea. They'll be told not to stick out their tongue, roll their eyes, frown, pout, or grit their teeth and make an angry face when told they couldn't do something. All of this is pretty good advice because none of those "faces" really helps us make and keep friends.

In this lesson, I want to talk about the kinds of facial expressions that do help us when it comes to having friends—ones when we're nodding, smiling, and looking or talking with enthusiasm. Or ones that help us show some sympathy or compassion when someone is talking about something that was unpleasant or difficult for them. Facial expressions do a lot to forge bonds between people. A lot of people, including kids with attention-deficit/hyperactivity disorder (ADHD), are not too good at that.

Now pretty much all of us have been in a situation in which we've had no idea what to talk about. It could be a company picnic or a neighborhood block party. It could be standing in line to pick up your child after school or sitting in the stands at a softball or baseball game. It could be at the cafeteria at work or school; at a PTA meeting, some community event, or fundraiser; or anywhere people are in close proximity for more than a few seconds. Pretty soon, that uncomfortable feeling starts to settle in, and you realize that you have no idea what to say. Ever caught a glimpse of your face as all of this was going on? If you've got nothing in mind to talk about, conversation will be pretty lame, and your face will look blank—and this doesn't inspire people to want to hang out with you.

Kids with ADHD have the same kind of problem when they try to have conversations. Part of the problem is that they can't think of the right words to say. But a more serious problem also gets in the way. As they're trying to think of what to say, their eyes don't focus on other people, and their faces look blank. Then they either say nothing or ramble on and on about stuff that no one cares about, and the chance to build a friendship through conversation gets lost.

The same thing happens when a child with ADHD is being asked to listen. Too often, the child says nothing back about what is being said, introduces another topic, and is looking at everything but the other person. This is a big turnoff—another chance to build a friendship through conversation gets lost.

Way too often, this pattern of not looking at others during conversation will continue throughout a child's life. Probably one of the biggest problems in the marriages of men with ADHD is that their spouses get the feeling that they don't care because they don't talk to them and don't look at them during conversations. In this lesson, we'll begin to work on changing that pattern.

THREE SKILLS FOR BETTER COMMUNICATION

When I teach children with ADHD how to have conversations, I focus on three parts. First, *it's important to have something to talk about.* That's why in the last lesson I shared some ideas on ways to help children figure out the interests of others, to practice their detective skills with their family and other kids, and to deliberately prepare for the day's conversations by thinking of three stories they could share. If you have something in mind to say, it will be easier for you to look at the other person during conversations.

Second, *it's important to be able to say what you want to say relatively quickly.* That's why in the last lesson, we talked about playing word-finding games and practicing at home on a daily basis. Although some might argue that it is critical for our nation's world status that we teach every child advanced mathematics, I would propose that it is actually more important for our children to remember important "people" facts so that they can learn how to have conversations. If we can figure out how to get ourselves inspired to help our children understand the "why"s of mathematics, let's hope we can help them learn the "how"s of conversations. In some ways, what we're trying to do is teach our kids a foreign language, only in this case, the words themselves are not brand new. They already know how to use their words to get certain basic needs met, but they may not know how to use their words for the purpose of connecting with others.

Take a moment to think about how you are teaching kids the foreign language called conversation. I know that there are all sorts of polls and surveys about how much time parents and children spend talking with each other. Truth is, the only survey that matters is the one that asks you one simple question: "How much time do you spend having conversations with your child?" If you're running with the majority, you might find that you're only spending about 7 minutes a day talking with your child (and much of that is spent on instructions and directions). I can't imagine any of us learning a foreign language in 7 minutes a day, so it shouldn't be a surprise that kids with ADHD aren't.

Some people may argue that children get all sorts of modeling in how to have conversations from television and movies, watching YouTube, spending time on Facebook, and texting each other. It may be true that these activities help a child learn what other kids might be interested in or like to talk about. Unfortunately, none of these experiences actually requires children to organize their ideas while they are involved in a conversation. And when watching videos, checking out Instagram, texting, or posting on Facebook, eye contact isn't part of the equation. Without those aspects of communication, watching TV, texting, or posting on Facebook won't help build conversational skills any more than writing a letter would because the child isn't *talking* and isn't learning how to read the facial expressions of others (and how to give an "I'm interested" look).

This is where you, other children, and other adults become critically important because you (and other people in a life skills group) can help your child get comfortable looking at the person he or she is talking with. You can help your child get better at showing some kind of sign that says, "I'm interested in what you're saying." You can help your child give some kind of facial expression that says, "I like talking with you." You can help your child figure out interesting topics to discuss. The simple, sad truth is that the child with ADHD who looks everywhere but at the person speaking, has no idea what to talk about, shows no sign of interest, and gives no indication of "I like you" isn't going to make or keep many friends.

In this class, we'll begin to help kids learn the third skill for better communication: During conversations, *facial expressions matter.* I remember one little guy whose parents were upset because he would look at everything but their faces when they were talking to him. One day, this family was at my clinic for a session, and the exasperated dad said to his son, "WHY DON'T YOU LOOK AT ME WHEN I'M TALKING WITH YOU?" Without pausing, his son said (about as matter-of-factly as possible), "Dad, you hear with your ears, not your eyes." Pretty obvious, right?

One of the lessons I ended up teaching this little boy is that we look at people not to hear them better but to let them know that we are interested and care. People like to be noticed when they speak and to feel like we care about what they are saying. That's part of the third skill of conversations that we teach our patients: Look at the person you're talking with to get across the idea that you like, care about, and are interested in him or her.

Now, there are a variety of ways that we can show we're interested and care. How we do that may need to change depending on the situation and our cultural background. Teaching our kids about such nuances will take time, but it's important and can save your kids some uncomfortable moments. Like the one I'm about to tell you about.

One of my sons, Diego, has a friend who got into trouble this year for doing something that some kids will do: address adults by their first name. This boy was walking down the hallway and saw the principal. The principal is a friendly, engaging man. So as the little boy approached the principal, he smiled, said "hi," and called the principal by his first name. Not the end of the world, but in the "school culture," it's not OK. The little boy ends up losing recess time for "being friendly." Unfortunately, he was using a facial expression with matching friendly words that was fine with kids and some adults, but not in "school world." So teaching our kids that context matters is important too.

FINE-TUNING CONVERSATIONS
SO THAT THEY WORK IN REAL LIFE

The last lesson was a warm-up for building connections for our kids and others. It was meant to help children begin to notice the interests of others so that they'd have a way to get into conversations. I hope your child has started to have small conversations with you, other family members, and the kids in his or her group or social network. So far, these were pretty staged conversations, using a small group of topics that the kids generated on a worksheet. We were working on discovering interests, likes, dislikes, good and bad moments, and sharing some of ours, which is a good place to start.

Now it's time to do a little fine-tuning to help our kids make the transition to real-life conversations. Even though YouTube, television shows, movies, and other types of entertainment don't help us speak, it can be helpful to watch a little of what's pouring out on the screens when you're looking for models of what to do or not do in conversations. I remember the first time that I saw the movie *Despicable Me* with my wife and my youngest boys. In one part of the story, a little girl who is an orphan is now living with a villain named Gru. Unfortunately, Gru has agreed to raise this girl and her sisters for sinister reasons. He thinks they can help him snatch a shrink-ray weapon from another bad guy. But as he's raising these little girls, something happens: He falls in love with them.

In one scene, Gru is helping one of the girls, Agnes, practice reciting a poem for her class. It's about a mother. The little girl is having problems with this because she doesn't remember her mother and really hasn't felt a mother's (or father's) love. The first time she reads her poem, it's dreadful. She uses a monotone voice, has a flat facial expression, and the speed and cadence of her words is robotic. No matter how many times Gru has her repeat the words, there's no change. Agnes keeps looking like a statue while speaking in a monotone, robotic voice.

In the rest of the movie, this same little girl is talking up a storm. She's full of life and is just joyous. How can that be? From my perspective, it's fairly simple. When Agnes is talking about something she knows and feels a connection with, it goes great. When she's trying to talk about something she doesn't know anything about, she's blank. The same is true of kids with ADHD. Kids might know all about Marvel Superheroes, *Star Wars*, or Ninjago, and they can talk your ear off if you happen to be interested in one of those. When children talk about something they know and like, their faces are highly animated and their voices change in tone as they describe, with great excitement, a particular movie scene. However, if it comes to having conversations about the interests of other kids or something another child saw or did, they are speechless; if they do talk, they sound and appear to be bored or detached.

As you begin to think about how to help a child develop conversation skills, there are several problems that need to be overcome. We need to help them think about something to say after "Hey," "What's up?" or "How's it going?" And this isn't easy. We need to help them prepare for conversations in different situations: waiting for the bus or riding to school; walking into school or standing at the locker; on the way to class or in the lunchroom; or maybe during karate class or when going to or coming from band, dance, baseball, soccer, football, or some other kind of group practice. In other words, we've got to prepare them for a variety of places where conversations will come up. And as all of this is going on, we've got to help them begin to look like they are actually interested in, like, and want to be friends with their conversation partners. This is not an easy task, but it is definitely doable.

TIPS FOR TEACHING KIDS TO HAVE CONVERSATIONS

As you teach this lesson, you might find it helpful to divide it into three parts. The first part focuses on helping children have fun playing around with different facial expressions during conversations. The second part teaches kids how to start conversations with others. The third part gives the child the chance to practice keeping conversations going in different social situations. During each of these parts, you can demonstrate "boring" and "interested" faces and ways to show enthusiasm.

I've learned that when I teach conversation skills, it's rare that we'll accomplish all the goals in a single class. As you practice these lessons with your class or child, you might find that it would be helpful to repeat them several times so your child can experience success in conversations before moving on.

I've provided a sample handout at the end of this lesson that you might find useful. It refers to the movie that I mentioned, *Despicable Me*, but you can adapt it for any movie or clips from two different movies that show flat versus animated voices and faces in conversations. I'll also use various scenes from *Star Wars* movies or other high-action adventure movies and ask the kids to point out what's missing in the characters' facial expressions (for example, in *Star Wars*, the characters rarely, if ever, smile).

Another resource you might use along with the worksheet (especially for Part 2) is reality TV. Yes, I said reality TV. Even though a lot of editing goes into producing these so-called unscripted shows, it's not hard to see that a lot of talking is going on to fill the time between action segments or family blowups. I find there can be a lot to learn from watching reality TV stars talk.

For example, one of my sons' favorite television shows is *Call of the Wildman*. My kids and I call it "Turtle Man" because that's the hero's nickname. In *Call of the Wildman*, each story is about a man named Ernie who goes into all sorts of dangerous situations and rescues animals who've gotten into places that people would rather them not be. One show is about a raccoon that's broken into a movie theater and is snacking on all the candy and popcorn. Another is about a huge rattlesnake that's hidden itself among a pile of clothes in a basement.

No matter what the situation, Turtle Man just walks up, asks the people what's going on, and starts to rescue the animal. Much of the action in this show is pretty amazing, as this guy removes snapping turtles, snakes, and other animals that can put a bite on you barehanded.

The interesting part for me (besides the exciting rescues) is that Turtle Man is very good at having conversations. As he's driving along with his buddy, they're busy talking about whatever they've seen or done, or getting ready to see or do. And these conversations happen in all sorts of places.

There are lots of other kinds of television shows that provide the same kind of chance for kids to learn about conversations. Each generation of kids seems to have their favorite. I can remember watching shows like *Full House, Fresh Prince of Bel-Air*, and *Saved by the Bell*. Today, there are a number of similar programs on the Disney Channel, PBS, and Nickelodeon. Shows like *Jessie, Girl Meets World, Liv and Maddie*, and *Austin and Ally* feature kids in real-life situations having conversations about all sorts of topics. There's also a cartoon version of an adventuring pair of brothers who teach kids about nature and animals, called *Wild Kratts*, that my sons really like.

It's not likely that these shows will be among the favorites of your child or teenager who has ADHD. Kids with ADHD tend to watch high-action shows. But I think you'll find that if you have a bit of a family TV time, when you all sit and watch a show like *Jessie* and talk about what's happening on the screen, you'll have a lot of laughs, and your child may learn a thing or two about having conversations.

As with each of the other lessons, it's fun to end this one with a game. It's a simple one, but it works great. We've all played it. It's a staring contest. Partners stare into each other's eyes until someone looks away or blinks. The first one who looks away or blinks loses. If you are playing this in a class, keep going until only two kids remain. The winner of the final matchup wins the prize.

Worksheet for Life Lesson 7: Sometimes Making Faces Can Be a Good Idea

Have you ever heard an adult say, "LOOK AT ME WHEN I'M TALKING TO YOU" or remind you to "LOOK AT ME WHEN YOU'RE SPEAKING"? For some kids, looking at the person they're talking or listening to is easy. For most kids, that's hard. After all, you hear with your ears, not your eyes . . . so what difference does it make if you look at them when they're talking or not?

Truth is, people like you to look at them for a few reasons. It gives them the idea that you are interested in them. It gives them the idea that you're interested in what they're talking about. And most important, by giving people the sense that you're interested in them or what they're talking about, they enjoy the conversation and like being with you . . . and that helps to build friendships, which all of us like.

So today, let's start to work on getting better at that "I like you" look. Here are some fun exercises to try.

PART 1: MOVIE TIME!

1. Watch the scene from *Despicable Me 2* where Agnes is rehearsing the Mother's Day poem she's been assigned to recite for school.
2. How did Agnes do? Does Agnes look at Gru? Does her face say, "Wow, look at me, listen-up, what I'm going to tell you about is really great"? No . . . of course not.
3. Now, pair up with someone and tell them something that happened to you. Use the robot voice and blank face, just like Agnes. Try it . . . don't be shy.
4. Now that your face is frozen, try to get it moving again. Watch the clip from *Despicable Me* where Gru wins a huge, stuffed unicorn for Agnes. Look at Agnes's face now and listen to her voice when she's talking.
5. How did Agnes do this time? Did she look at Gru? Did her face say, "Wow, look at me, listen-up, what I'm going to tell you about is really great"?

Worksheet for Life Lesson 7: Sometimes Making Faces Can Be a Good Idea *(Continued)*

6. Now it's your turn. Think for a minute about something that you saw, something that you heard about, or something that you did that you thought was pretty neat. Got an idea? Okay, now try telling someone else about it.

Before you start, pause, think about what you want to tell the other kid, and then start your conversation. You might say:

Hey, did you know that _____
    happened today?
Hey, today I saw that _____
    happened.
Hey did you hear that _____
    happened?

Whatever you go with, try to do it two ways, first . . . do it the boring way. Make it as horribly boring as you can. For your second take, try it with some excitement. Do your best to get across the idea that whatever you saw, heard about, or did, it was great.

PART 2: "LIVE ACTION!" TIME

For this activity, you and a partner will act out an everyday situation where you're just talking. You don't need or want anything in particular from the other kid. You're just passing the time and maybe getting to know the other person a little bit. This is a time when you could bring up a story of something that happened to you or you heard about or saw. You could pretend that the conversation is happening while you're waiting for the bus. Or you're on the bus. Or hanging around at school. Or at lunch.

After you've practiced a couple of situations, think about what you've learned.

1. Are you pretty good at looking at other kids when they're talking?

_____

(continued)

Worksheet for Life Lesson 7: Sometimes Making Faces Can Be a Good Idea (*Continued*)

2. Are you pretty good at looking at other kids when you're talking?

   _____

3. Are you pretty good at sounding excited when they're talking?

   _____

4. Are you pretty good at sounding excited when you're talking?

   _____

5. Can you think of things to talk about pretty easily?

   _____

If any of these are a problem for you, practice during the week. For example, when you watch TV, really focus on how the characters behave. Do they look at each other? How do they show enthusiasm or act interested? Another way to practice would be to agree with your family that every night at dinner, each person gets a turn to start up a conversation about something they think other people would like to talk about. Just like learning anything new, it takes time. Practice about 15 minutes a day if you can, but remember that any amount of time is better than nothing.

IGNORING TEASING WILL NOT MAKE IT GO AWAY

One of the saddest and most confusing moments for us happens when our child comes home from school in tears, upset because of something another kid said or did. Sometimes it's a threat that another child is going to beat them up. Sometimes it's being shunned by a group of kids who won't let your child sit or play a game with them. Sometimes it's getting laughed at because a child looks different, lacks athletic abilities, needs glasses or braces, or doesn't wear the "right" kind of clothes or own the newest electronic toy. It starts with a little verbal push that we sometimes call teasing, but more accurately it is called *bullying*. The simple truth about bullying is this: If the push is ignored, the attack will just get more and more intense.

As a parent, you have encountered kids who have been mean to your child and struggled to decide what to do. If you haven't dealt with this yet, you're lucky. Kids with attention-deficit/hyperactivity disorder (ADHD) will often do more poorly when it comes to learning basic math facts . . . and other kids will notice. Kids with ADHD will be slower to finish their seatwork . . . and other students will notice. Kids with ADHD won't pay attention to the teacher, or will speak out in class and be repeatedly corrected by the teacher . . . and other students will notice. On the playground, kids with ADHD may lose their focus during a game and cause their team to lose . . . and that will be noticed, too. Pretty soon, your child starts to hear that he's stupid or a "retard." Maybe you sought the help of your school and got some temporary relief, or maybe not. In any event, one truth remains: As much as we wish we could be with our children at all times to protect them, we can't. Until a child learns how to face and address teasing from others, their life can be a nightmare.

I have no idea who came up with the saying "Sticks and stones may break my bones but words will never hurt me." However, one thing that I am certain about is that whoever first said it surely wasn't living in the 21st century. Maybe in the days of your great-grandparents, who might have lived miles away from their nearest neighbor, it didn't matter if someone didn't have a good opinion of you. Maybe in the days when you had to share a phone line with a dozen or so other families, it didn't matter. However, in a time when you can discover somebody's negative opinion of you on Facebook, in a text message, or in a harassing phone call that can come any time of day or night, it can get to you. I'm guessing that if you only saw someone you didn't like once a week or so or for a few minutes of "unsupervised time" at school, you could ignore it. But in today's world, if people decide they don't like you and want to make your life miserable, they can do it 24-7. If this becomes a problem for you and your child, you'll need to decide together how you want to take on this challenge.

In decades past, parents were told to tell children to "just ignore it" when they were teased. I guess the idea was that if you ignored teasing, it would just go away. But that runs counter to the biological imperative to establish our dominance and seek the best place in the pack. Even though we don't head out into the fields or woods and shake our antlers and bump into each other like deer, we have developed other, supposedly less painful ways to put us on top and other people below us. Some people seek to prove their superiority in the classroom, others on a ball field, others in a dance competition, or in any of the other types of activities in which we get rated, a rank is assigned, and you find out where you stand in the pack. In general, people seem to be accepting of that "more civilized" process for establishing rank.

Whether or not you like it, this process of being ranked surrounds your child, and it contributes to the development of her sense of confidence. Children are graded in school based on their knowledge. Those who are ranked high grow a bit in confidence by realizing that they are "good" at academics. Other children get selected for games in the order of their ability or social desirability. They grow a bit in confidence by realizing that they are liked and are considered to be good at something by their peers.

HOW BULLYING STARTS

Throughout all of this activity to get that feeling of "I'm good at something that matters," another option is lurking in the background: the use of verbal and physical intimidation to put others below you on a little speck of turf called school. There's been a lot of research done on bullying, which may or may not interest you. I put it this way for the kids I teach at my clinic: Bullies are "hurting" kids who try to feel better about themselves by trying to make you feel bad about being you. Somewhere in their lives they forgot all that kindergarten advice about being kind, patient, generous, and tolerant with others.

It's kind of strange how this happens, because hanging out with other kids starts off pretty decently. Nursery school and preschool are often pretty good places for kids. There are usually a lot of grown-ups around and lots of fun stuff to do. Everyone's supposed to be learning about being nice, taking turns, sharing, and being kind. If you push someone to get a toy, or if you don't share and you take all the crayons for yourself, you'll be told that's not a good idea. The television shows you watch tell you that everybody's special, and the characters treat each other with kindness and respect. Day after day, the child hears these messages.

What most kids don't learn early on, however, is the more proactive social skills. For instance, how to welcome new people into your group. I'll never forget when my wife and I were out "shopping" for the perfect preschool for our two youngest sons, Diego and Julian. The boys were born in Guatemala and have a darker skin color than ours. In our little dream world, this perfectly accepting, multicultural preschool would include teachers who always smiled and kids who were all busily working on being generous, learning to share, and, most of all, being kind.

That image was quickly shattered at one of the preschools we visited. The teacher asked us loudly in front of the class, "Now where did *your* boys come from?" and "Do they speak English?" (without asking our boys a single question). As we walked out the door, the teacher exclaimed to her class, "Well isn't that interesting? We've never had a Diego in our class before." Now our boys were oblivious to all of this and skipped merrily to the car. As I glanced back to take a final look at the school, I saw all the boys in the class lined up at the window, sticking their tongues out at our kids. Lacking the skill of welcoming others warmly, and in this case subtly aided by their teacher's model, kids can easily default to that "top-dog" instinct, even if they might be good at sharing toys and taking turns. Welcome to reality!

When kids arrive at kindergarten, they'll face situations they've never encountered before. The values they've been hearing about at home, school, day care, recreational centers, and church will be put to the test from the beginning of their entry into kindergarten. It wasn't until kindergarten that my boys had to face bullying themselves and figure out how to deal with it. Within the first week of school, I received some news that stunned me. My son Julian was sitting next to a boy at lunch. The boy said to my son, "I bet I can make you cry." Julian just looked at him, confused, and said, "No you can't." The boy then proceeded to punch my son in the nose!

Now, the school did what would be expected. The other boy was corrected, and efforts were made to comfort my son. But Julian's world was forever changed. Within a week, all of the "I love you, you love me" stuff that he learned in preschool went out the window. My son realized that the new world of school contained dangers he had never faced before. Now he would experience challenges that we should have expected but never believed would happen, at least not in the first week of kindergarten.

But the story doesn't end there. Other kids were nearby and watched the whole scene as it unfolded, including my other son, Diego. It probably won't surprise you to hear that not a single child spoke up—not a single child did anything. They watched. They all participated in the weekly antibullying programs that taught them about respecting others and being kind. But the take-home message was that there were children at school who would hurt you for no particular reason.

In the weeks after this event, other children experienced some version of what Julian got in Week 1. Again, the members of the school staff did what they needed to do. Teachers were alerted when the aggression occurred, met with students, and discussed how to handle things. The child who had acted aggressively was disciplined. But the ripple effect had begun.

At recess time, kids would still run around, hang on climbers, and do the usual playground stuff. But because they had seen unprovoked aggression, they now had to decide how to protect themselves. Not surprisingly, some of the kids ended up teaming up with the boy who had "begun" the aggression, including Julian's brother, Diego.

Diego is a little, speedy boy who loves to run and run and run. In his early years, I think his favorite thing to do was just run with other kids, checking to make sure that he was the fastest. One day, my wife and I decided to have lunch with the boys at school. Afterward, we took a few moments to observe the boys at playground from our car. We were shocked to see what happened.

Pretty quickly, we spotted Diego running around as usual. But we saw something that confused us. Diego was running with other kids, but it looked like the pack ran into another boy and knocked him down. The next thing we saw was another boy getting on top of the kid on the ground . . . and my son just watching. We started to jump out of the car and head for the playground, but one of the playground monitors was already on her way.

As the monitor was moving toward the boys, I saw Diego slipping away from the group. The monitor interviewed the boys and took away the one who was on top of the other boy. And the games continued.

After school, we talked with Diego about this. At first, he said that the other kid was accidentally pushed to the ground. This would have made sense, except for one detail. Diego didn't reach down to help the other child. And when the other boy got on top of the kid who had fallen, Diego hadn't done anything to help. That just wasn't like our son. After a bunch of "I don't know" explanations, Diego finally told us. "Mom, Dad, I didn't want to get hurt like Julian did. So I did what the other kids told me to do."

After speaking with Diego, we insisted that he let the school know that he was part of the group of kids who hurt another little boy (and face those consequences). We also asked him to write a note to the other boy, apologizing for what he had done and promising him that he wouldn't do it again. We also told him that he needed to do something nice for the other boy to make up for making his day scary and that we would ask him to tell us what he did after school the next day. Fortunately, this didn't happen again.

The stories of Julian and Diego notwithstanding, most children in kindergarten are not prone to physical aggression. The other kids quickly learn who the aggressive kids are and that they don't have to be intimidated by them because usually there is enough supervision around to keep the children safe. In addition, most kindergarten children think it's a big deal if you have to go to the principal or your parents get called to school. So the pushing and hitting problem is addressed pretty quickly and effectively during the primary grades.

WHAT BULLYING LOOKS LIKE AFTER KINDERGARTEN

Unfortunately, the same is not necessarily true for the mean talk that starts up in second or third grade. This is when kids seem to notice differences more, and the teasing becomes more complex than "I bet I can make you cry." What's worse is that the adults who were ever-hovering in kindergarten to break up scuffles aren't always able to detect mean talk. Talk can stay below the surface and may never turn into a scuffle. Even though none of us like to be teased, made fun of, or talked to in a cruel, insensitive way, we kind of expect it as a part of life. Unless you're living in some idyllic community, chances are you've been teased or spoken to in a mean way.

The first thing you can do when talking with your child about teasing is to let him or her know that it's a fact of life. My sense is that we all get teased about something, for whatever reason. If you happen to be pretty, you can get teased for that, courtesy of someone who is jealous of you. If you aren't someone who is considered "pretty," you'll face teasing by the beauty queens who want to ensure their status at school. If you happen to be a great baseball player, you can be teased for that, courtesy of someone who wished they were pitching instead of you. Then again, if you're lousy at baseball, someone will make fun of you for that. If you happen to be tall, you can get teased for that. If you are short, that can be the focus of your teasing. If you're smart, you can get teased for being a "brainiac." Then again, if you're not considered smart, you'll face teasing for that. No matter who you are, no matter what abilities or traits you possess, someone will find a way to tease you. And you will either develop a strategy for handling that or you'll be pretty miserable.

It can also help to share a story with your child about your own experience with teasing, especially if you found a strategy for avoiding the worthless feeling that can come along with it. If you don't have such a story from your life, feel free to use mine. Here's my first experience being teased. It happened for me in the third grade. I was this kid who had allergies, but in the days before Benadryl, Claritin-D, Allegra, and the other medicines that could stop a runny nose, I was armed with a handkerchief (a little square piece of cloth that kids used in the days before disposable tissues). For much of the year, I was fine. However, in springtime, I was a drippy mess. So I spent a lot of time blowing my nose endlessly into this little square that was soaked by midmorning.

Needless to say, in the world of third graders, that was "noticed." Then someone came up with the name "Snot-rag." Pretty soon, everyone was calling me "Snot-rag," like it was my first name, and laughing about it.

So what were my options? I could have punched the other kids, but then I'd be in trouble. I could have teased them back, but I had been taught that wasn't right either so I'd get in trouble for that. I tried saying nothing and acting like it didn't bother me. But it did. And then, I had my "light bulb" moment.

For whatever reason, the truth about my situation hit me. It was true that I had a runny nose. It was true, that I always carried a "snot rag." It was true that I used my snot rag a lot. But there was one thing that wasn't true: I WASN'T A SNOT RAG!

The next time someone came up to me and called me "Snot-rag," I reached into my back pocket, pulled out my handkerchief, and calmly said, "Here you go" and started to give him my drippy handkerchief. The kid was obviously grossed out, and yelled out, "Hey, what are you doing? Stop!" I said, "What's wrong? You asked for my snot rag." He said, "No I didn't, I called *you* a snot rag." I smiled and jokingly said, "No, I'm not a snot rag, this is. You sure you don't want it?" The other kids laughed, I laughed, he walked away, and that was the end of it.

HOW TO DEFUSE TEASING AND DISARM BULLIES

Without realizing it, I had stumbled onto the keys for what to do when I was being teased. Here they are:

First, I needed to be able to recognize the truth about what was being said, which was I really did have a drippy nose and needed to use a handkerchief a lot.

Second, I had to realize that having a constantly runny nose didn't make me defective. No one's perfect. We've all got our downsides.

Third, I had to fight the urge to be mean back. Even though I'm pretty good at coming up with stuff to say, I'd been taught that wasn't right. Teasing back also just makes the situation worse.

Fourth, instead of being sarcastic or mean in return, I discovered that if I could accept the truth, and could admit that with a face and tone that said, "I'm not afraid of you, I'm not mad at you, but I don't want to play the teasing game," things worked out pretty well.

So one part of stopping teasing in life has to do with learning how to accept the truth about our little weaknesses and act in a way that says, "I'm not scared or mad, and I don't want to play the teasing game." Even though this will work out better than saying nothing, crying, getting mad, or teasing back, this strategy won't work all by itself. Remember all those lessons about building confidence and the importance of facing fears, having friends, and getting good at something that matters to kids your child's age? Those are important too. No matter how many times you try to teach your child to say something brave to a bully, unless he is growing in confidence by facing fears, getting good at something that matters, and developing a group of friends, he's still going to come across as weak and is likely to return home crushed and upset. Even though every school in our country must have policies to help protect that children from being teased (and you should inform the school if your child is being teased), no system is perfect, and your child is still likely to have to address some form of teasing anyway.

Let's look at another example to see this approach in action. One of my sons came home after school telling me that a kid made fun of where he was from. It seems that one of the kids in his class jokingly said he was from "guacamole" instead of Guatemala. Julian had no idea what guacamole was, but he knew he was being teased. I could have told my son to ignore it—no big deal, right? Instead, I talked about the truth. I explained to Julian that guacamole was made from squashed avocados, tasted pretty good, and people put it in burritos and also dip chips in it. My son was like "Really? That's what they call that stuff?"

When we "practiced" what to say, we first went back to the "truth" part. The truth is, he was born in Guatemala, not guacamole; guacamole is something you eat. So the next time the other kid teasingly said he was from Guacamole, my son learned to say some version of, "Nope, I was born in Guatemala. Guacamole is something you eat," smile kindly, and just walk away. We practiced that at home, he tried it out at school, and it worked.

WHEN BULLYING BECOMES SERIOUS

Fortunately, my son has friends, is generally liked, will face fears, and is getting good at stuff that matters to kids his age. But what about children who don't have those things on their side? What if they don't have many (or any) friends? What if they tend to avoid what they fear, rather than face it? What if every time they check on Facebook, someone's posting some nasty stuff about them? What if they get text messages that are just flat-out cruel? School and law enforcement agencies need to be informed because they can and should be involved in deterring such actions. If you suspect that cyber-bullying is part of the problem, act immediately to help your child. We have all heard about tragedies that occur when parents, friends, school officials, and law enforcement agencies ignore such bullying. Schools now have established policies that result in significant disciplinary actions and other types of interventions when cyber-bullying occurs. Take the time to learn what policies have been established in your school district and how to get help if this is part of the cause of your child's anxiety and depression. However, even with such help from you and the school, your child will need to learn to develop friendships, face fears, and respond to bullying using the kinds of techniques presented in this lesson.

WHAT IF YOUR CHILD IS THE BULLY?

When a parent discovers that his or her child is the one doing the bullying, it can be equally shocking. Just like the parent of the child being bullied, you might want to pretend that it's no big deal. That it's just part of growing up and everybody does it. Although that may be true (that most people tease and are teased), children who establish themselves as one of the class bullies need help too.

There are several reasons kids become bullies. Sometimes it's because they are the youngest child in a family of kids who are pretty aggressive toward them. Their older sibs taunt, put down, and assault them at home on a daily basis. Sometimes their siblings will say that they're doing it to "toughen up" their brother or sister. Sometimes these older siblings are taking out some of the physical punishment they've received at home on their little brother or sister. These kids get skilled at fighting and saying mean stuff, and take out the hurt they feel on their classmates. They may or may not form cliques and exclude others. More likely, they will be pretty tough "loners" that other kids stay away from.

Other kids who become bullies do it because it makes them feel they are better than others. It's that drive to be the top dog (or

137

queen bee) taken to extremes. Although these kids can be physically aggressive, this type of bully usually creates cliques of other kids who make the lives of others miserable. They will constantly single out others and taunt them, mock them, and tease them. This type of bullying is more common among girls.

The other kind of bully is the bystander. I consider kids who simply watch or join the bullying tactics of others to be bullies too. Although they might not initiate the bullying, their attention and support keeps it going. Bystanders usually tell me that they don't say anything because they don't want to be the next target.

So if any of these descriptions sound like your child, you can do a lot to help. If the issue is some too-tough siblings, you might find it helpful to have some family meetings and use some of the strategies I've shared with you (Positive Practice, Positive Punishment, Time Stands Still) to help your children learn some new ways of living together. If your child is not involved in activities that can build confidence, now would be a good time to start. Some of the lessons on appreciation and kindness that I'll talk about later in this book may also be helpful. If these kinds of strategies do not seem to be enough, this would be another issue to review with your child's physician and therapist.

TEACHING TIPS FOR DEALING WITH TEASING AND BULLYING

As I mentioned earlier, when talking to your child about teasing, it's good to emphasize that teasing is pretty common, and it's one way that some kids try to feel good about themselves. You can also get into some version of the Animal Planet explanation about deer, rhinos, and other creatures pushing away at each other and locking horns to determine rank, emphasizing that we are people, not deer, and we've been taught better ways to feel good about ourselves.

Next, try to generate as many situations as possible when teasing happens and see if you and your child can identify the common denominator among them. In the life skills class I teach, we establish a comprehensive "greatest hits" list of ways that kids tease other kids and practice figuring out what the "truth" is behind each one.

Finally, describe for your child the four-step strategy for taking on teasing, and see if you can role-play some scenarios using these steps to counteract teasing in the situations you generated. In my clinic, we practice in parent–child teams as well as kid-to-kid teams. The goal is to be able to develop some comfort and confidence in responding to teasing statements without resorting to being mean or threatening to others.

To help teach this lesson, consider using the worksheet at the end of this lesson. Once your child has filled in the blanks and planned out some responses to the things others tease him or her about, practice the planned responses with some role-plays. If your child needs to warm up first with insults that aren't so close to home, start role-playing using the Top Ten insults at their school.

In a life skills class setting, games can be a fun way to reinforce what we practiced. This game is pretty simple. I ask the kids to turn over their worksheet, and I call out an insult. Kids have 90 seconds to write down as many responses as they can think of. Sarcastic comments, insults, teasing back, or threatening the other kid doesn't count. The child with the highest number of constructive, tease-defusing responses is the winner. Because kids with ADHD often have difficulty writing quickly, I'll let parents or guardians record answers if that is easier, but of course the kids have to come up with the answers themselves.

Worksheet for Life Lesson 8: Ignoring Teasing Will Not Make It Go Away

Everybody gets teased sometimes. So what can you do? Here are four steps you can try when you are teased.

First, you need to be able to recognize the truth about what was being said. Let's say you get a really bad grade on a math test. Another kid notices it, laughs, and calls you "Stupid." So, what does the truth sound like? It could be "I hate it when I get a sucky grade." It could be "Yeah, math *is* really hard for me." What would you say?

Here's another example. Let's say someone calls you a loser because your parents don't have enough money to buy you the most popular kinds of clothes. What's the truth sound like? Is it, "Yep, we don't have the money to buy $200 sneakers"? What would you say?

Second, you need to realize that agreeing with the truth that you're not perfect doesn't make you worse than somebody else. We've all got our downsides.

Third, you have to fight the urge to be mean back. Even if you're pretty good at coming up with stuff to say back, that's like pouring gasoline on the fire. Most of the time, we're just teased because somebody wants to play the reindeer antler pushing game with us. Once you start teasing back, they have even more reason to keep it up.

Fourth, instead of being sarcastic or mean in return, you need to discover a way of looking and a tone of voice after being teased that says "I'm not afraid of you, I'm not mad at you, but I don't want to play the teasing game." The goal here is to show strength but not meanness. If you were called "Gigantor" because you are so tall and your answer was some version of "Yep, tall genes run in my family," what else is there to say? Without saying it, you're calmly asking the other kid some version of "That's true . . . and your point is?"

Now the other kid may want to push around a little more, but the game's over. You showed that you could accept the truth, that you weren't scared, that the other kid isn't better than you, and that you don't

Worksheet for Life Lesson 8: Ignoring Teasing Will Not Make It Go Away (*Continued*)

want to push back and forth and play the teasing game. You can now just walk away to be with your friends or do something you'd rather do. If the other kid keeps it up, threatens to hurt you, or starts to get physical, tell an adult because there really is something wrong with that child and he or she needs some help.

PRACTICE TIME!

The first step in dealing with teasing is to get good at accepting the truth of any put-down. To prepare for possible put-downs that might come your way, take a couple minutes to fill out the following list. Keep in mind that insults thrown at other people and not directly at you also count in the silly, move-to-the-top-of-the-heap game that kids play.

TOP 10 INSULT LIST

Here are the top 10 insults I hear at my school (directed either at me or someone else):

1. _____
2. _____
3. _____
4. _____
5. _____
6. _____
7. _____
8. _____
9. _____
10. _____

(continued)

Worksheet for Life Lesson 8: Ignoring Teasing Will Not Make It Go Away (*Continued*)

Now that you have your list, write down some of the ones that kids tease *you* about. Only this time, also write down what the "truth" is when it comes to you.

Here are some of the things kids say to tease me:

1. _____

   The truth is _____

2. _____

   The truth is _____

Finally, plan out what you will say to tell someone who's teasing you that it's GAME OVER. Practice role-playing your lines with someone else. Remember to use a tone of voice that is strong but free from sarcasm or meanness. If you have time, try to come up with some good responses to any of the Top 10 Insults so you can help out others next time they get teased.

_____

_____

_____

LIFE LESSON 9

EVERY DAY, FIND WAYS TO SHOW APPRECIATION

In the last several lessons, we've been talking about ways to help a child become more confident. I hope your child is growing in confidence by getting good at something that matters to others, is facing fears, and is making and keeping friends by sharing activities and having conversations. We also talked about ways to handle teasing. Now it's time to consider a totally different way to build confidence: doing what's right.

In Lesson 4, I mentioned Dr. Stanley Coopersmith's book *The Antecedents of Self-Esteem* and his reflections on the sources of confidence—being liked by others, being good at something, and believing you can succeed in difficult situations.[1] In this lesson, I want to highlight one additional factor: Confidence also comes from doing what a person believes is right. Dr. Coopersmith's position was that everyone has a "moral code," and our sense of confidence is linked to how well we follow that code. If we live our lives according to our moral code, we feel more confident. If we don't, our confidence decreases.

The struggle between doing what's right rather than what's wrong has been going on forever. People who read the Bible learn about Adam and Eve being told by God not to eat the fruit from a

---

[1] Coopersmith, S. (1981). *The antecedents of self-esteem* (2nd ed.). Palo Alto, CA: Consulting Psychologists Press.

143

specific tree in the Garden of Eden. Adam and Eve give in to their desire to taste the fruit, and really bad stuff happens to them. People who watch Disney movies see Pinocchio struggle with the temptation not to go to school. His conscience, in the form of Jiminy Cricket, reminds him to do the right thing, singing, "And always let your conscience be your guide." But Pinocchio ignores Jiminy's advice, goes off to Pleasure Island instead of going to school, and starts to turn into a donkey, just like the other kids who didn't do the right thing.

In every family, no matter what their religious beliefs are, kids first develop their own moral compass on the basis of what their family considers to be right and wrong. Even before language skills are fully developed, a moral code is being forged by parents, grandparents, and other guardians. A forceful "no" is expressed when a toddler decides to bite his sibling in retaliation for a stolen toy or when he or she darts into the street after a runaway ball.

WHO ARE YOUR CHILD'S TEACHERS?

Over the years, other teachers besides parents enter into the picture. Could be another kid, a schoolteacher, a religious leader, a karate instructor, a coach, a computer, an X-Box, the Internet, or even the ever-popular electronic "babysitter," the TV. In my house, I jokingly refer to the TV as "Tommy the TV." And I use the same rules for Tommy as anyone else who comes into our home: If anyone is showing and encouraging my kids to do stuff that I don't think is OK, they have to go home. If Tommy the TV is doing it, then Tommy gets turned off.

Early on in my sons' lives, I realized just how much of an influence the TV could have on the development of their values. One hot summer day, I was hanging out on the back deck with my then 5-year-old son, Jay. We were grilling burgers and hot dogs. All of a sudden, his sweet, innocent voice said, "Hey, Dad, something's missing."

"What's missing, Jay?" I asked him.

As matter-of-fact as could be, he replied, "Bud Light." Feeling stunned that my son was talking about beer, I asked him, "What's Bud Light?"

He shrugged and simply said, "I don't know, Dad, but on TV they always have it at barbeques."

Parents, ask yourself who's teaching the kids in your house.

One of the reasons that I'm particularly concerned about the impact of messages coming from our television sets and other entertainment media is that the TV doesn't recognize the age of its audience members or their tendencies. Children with attention-deficit/hyperactivity disorder (ADHD) tend to be impulsive, so glorifying the ability of awesomely strong actors to settle conflict in a highly aggressive way may not be the message you want delivered to your child. Similarly, because kids with ADHD (when untreated) have a much higher rate of alcohol and substance abuse, a TV commercial about how "natural" it is to have a Bud Light may not be what you want someone to teach your child.

One of the things I've learned as I've taught my life skills classes is that despite our differences, there are certain beliefs when it comes to right and wrong that are shared among various ethnic and religious groups. Generally, people will say it's good to be kind and bad to be cruel; good to be generous, bad to be selfish; good to be tolerant, bad to discriminate; good to be patient, bad to be impatient; good to look for the positives in others, bad to be critical. The list goes on and on. When I talk with kids and parents in my class, it's pretty clear that each family has a moral code.

GOING BEYOND THE MAGIC WORDS

It's also pretty clear that in many of the families I teach, focusing on what is "important, interesting, life threatening, or fun" can encourage them to forget about being generous, kind, patient, loving, and appreciative. And that can lead to a family experience in which parents feel unappreciated and unloved and kids feel like all that ever happens is that they get criticized for doing the wrong thing.

In this lesson, we begin to focus on growing in confidence by getting better at following our family's moral code. I start with showing appreciation, because everyone wants to be appreciated. The challenge is help children get into the habit of showing appreciation every day. More often than not, parents try to instill values such as honesty, sharing, and patience, overlooking the need to teach their children the importance of showing appreciation.

Think about it: How much time do you spend reminding your children to say *please* and *thank you*, and how much time do you spend teaching them to show appreciation beyond those situation-specific words? As long as we laser-focus on our children remembering to say the "magic words," we're missing out on the chance to teach so much more when it comes to appreciation.

Now, a simple *thank you* is fine as the start of showing appreciation. But children who simply learn to parrot the words *please* and *thank you* are missing the big picture. These kids inadvertently begin to develop a sense of entitlement and grow up thinking that their role in life is to be a recipient, rather than a provider, of love and kindness—"Here I am, Mom and Dad. Love me, feed me, clothe me, play with me, and buy me lots of stuff. And oh, yes, I'll try to remember to say thanks." If you fast-forward into the future, you often find that children raised to be "me thinkers" later become adults who don't understand how to be in healthy adult relationships in which focusing on the needs of their spouse and others is crucial. Learning how to show appreciation is key for healthy adult relationships.

When children are raised to think about others and show appreciation, the world they live in becomes a much better place. They become a positive love force rather than a consumer of love. What does this look like for your family? Well, it's possible that for your family, it's the difference between the child who wants to invite lots of kids so there will be more presents for her and the child who asks her friends not to bring gifts but instead to bring food for a homeless shelter or for an animal shelter. It's the difference between handing your child the money to buy a present on Mother's Day or Father's Day and the child who saves his allowance and buys his parent a ticket to see a favorite performer in concert. It's the difference between lugging in a week's supply of groceries while your kids watch TV and your children jumping up to help you carry in the bags.

How our children begin to become "me thinkers" or "us thinkers" depends on what we teach. One of the best perspectives on this process was described by Dr. Wess Stafford, the former CEO of Compassion International, a Christian organization devoted to rescuing children from the psychological, spiritual, physical, and educational consequences that can come from living in poverty. Dr. Stafford's perspective is unique in that he grew up spending much of his life as a missionary's child, where he was a member of a tribe living on the Ivory Coast of Africa.

Unlike child-rearing practices in more developed parts of the world, children living in some of the impoverished regions of Africa are valued for what they can contribute to their tribe today, as well as when they grow up. These children are not burdens to be put aside and occupied by television and other electronic devices. Instead, they help with all of the daily tasks to the degree that they can. Playtime occurs as part of work time. The tribe rests together at the end of the day, when the work is done.

Somehow we seem to have forgotten the talents and contributions that our kids can make to family life and taking care of family work. We make all the meals. We make the beds. We clean the house. We wash the clothes. We do it all while our children lounge around or play. And then we're surprised when they are unappreciative and self-absorbed. If the only thing you ask your child to do is to put out the garbage once per week, don't be surprised when he forgets. If you've conditioned your children to believe that they are only to be the recipients of love in a relationship, why would you expect them to do anything for you?

TIPS FOR TEACHING APPRECIATION

Somewhere along the line, we got fooled into thinking that the pursuit of our personal happiness meant to focus on "me" and what "I want." This message comes across boldly in the old adage "Whoever dies with the most stuff wins." This lesson is intended to give you and your child to chance to conduct a small experiment; in this lesson, you and your child will focus on experiencing what it feels like when you spend time thinking about others, rather than yourself.

To teach this lesson at home or in a class, set aside about half an hour. Tell your child some version of the following: "For the next half hour or so, we're going to check out what it feels like to spend time thinking about someone other than yourself. We all know what it's like to spend our days thinking about what *we* need or what we could do so that *we* feel good. Let's see what it feels like to spend our time focusing on helping someone else feel good."

To help you with this lesson, I've included some worksheets for you to use as you teach your child this important life lesson.

Child Worksheet for Life Lesson 9: Everyone Wants to Be Appreciated—Even Parents!

Appreciation is saying "thanks," but it is much more than that. It can be a hug "just because" (not only when your parent buys you something) or a time when you tell your parents what you really like and admire about them. Has it been a while since you did those things? Think about what you like about your parent or parents and complete these sentences:

1. I really like it when my parent _____

   _____ .

2. Even though I rarely say it, I've always noticed that my parent is very good at doing _____

   _____for me.

3. I really think it's neat that my parent can _____

   _____ .

4. Sometimes, late at night, I sit back, smile, and remember when my parent _____

   _____ .

5. I think it's really important that Mom (Dad) knows I admire her (him) for _____

   _____ .

6. It meant a lot to me when my parent _____

   _____ .

Now that you've had a couple of minutes to think about some of the reasons that you appreciate your parents, let them know. Share what you've written with your parent(s) and make it part of conversations that happen at home. Maybe you'll mention one of these things when your mom is frustrated about something she could have done better at work, or when your dad is worried about paying the bills or just seems down. Or maybe just surprise them with your kind words out of the blue!

Parent Worksheet for Life Lesson 9: Everyone Wants to be Appreciated, Even Kids!

Everyone wants to be appreciated, even your kids. They want to have the feeling that you notice what they do for you and that you are thankful for it. Has it been a while since you sat with your child and told them what you liked or admired about them? As you begin to think about the things that you appreciate about your child, complete these sentences:

1. I really like it when my child _____
   _____.

2. Even though I rarely say it, I've always noticed that my child is very good at doing _____
   _____ for me.

3. I think that it's really neat that my child can _____
   _____.

4. Sometimes, late at night, I sit back, smile and remember when my child
   _____
   _____.

5. I really think that it's important that my child knows that I admire them for _____
   _____.

6. It really meant a lot to me when my child _____
   _____.

Now that you've had a couple of minutes to think about how you appreciate your child, let them know. Take a few minutes and tell them the things you've written.

Child Worksheet for Life Lesson 9: How Well Do You Know Each Other?

How well do you and your parent know each other? The better you do, the easier it will be for you to show each other appreciation. Take some time to think about your parent, grandparent, or guardian and answer the following questions.

1. What is your parent's favorite TV show? _____
2. What is your parent's favorite room in the house? _____
3. What makes your parent angry? _____
4. What calms your parent down when he or she is angry? _____
5. What makes your parent feel sad? _____
6. What makes your parent feel better when he or she is sad? _____
7. What do you do that makes your parent feel proud? _____
8. What is your parent's favorite food? _____
9. What does your parent like to do for fun? _____
10. What is your parent's least favorite chore? _____
11. My parent would love it if I would: _____

Now check with your parent. How many did you get right? _____

Parent Worksheet for Life Lesson 9: How Well Do You Know Each Other?

How well do you and your child know each other? The better you do, the easier it will be for you to show each other appreciation. Take some time to think about your child and answer the following questions.

1. What is your child's favorite TV show? _____
2. What is your child's favorite room in the house? _____
3. What makes your child angry? _____
4. What calms your child down when he or she is angry? _____
5. What makes your child feel sad? _____
6. What makes your child feel better when he or she is sad? _____
7. What do you do that makes your child feel proud? _____
8. What is your child's favorite food? _____
9. What does your child like to do for fun? _____
10. What is your child's least favorite chore? _____
11. My child would love it if I would: _____

Now check with your child. How many did you get right? _____

After everyone finishes writing down answers, spend some time together reading your worksheets, and just laugh and enjoy this moment. For a lot of the kids and parents, they are hearing stuff that they'd been hoping to hear for a long time. If I'm teaching this lesson in a life skills class, I'll encourage the families to spend some time sharing with each other the things they learned. Then we shift into a game.

The game I pick for this lesson is meant to continue to strengthen the good feeling that comes from feeling close to your parent or guardian and your child. It's also meant to set the stage for our next lesson on the benefits of being kind. Often I'll have the parent and child working together on a balloon game in which the parent will toss three balloons in the air and the child has to keep them from touching the ground. We keep track of how many seconds the child can do that. Then the child will toss three balloons in the air, and the parent has to keep them from touching the ground. Again we keep track of how long the parent keeps the balloons afloat. We add up the total scores, and that's how we determine the winner of the game.

No matter who wins the game, everyone has experienced the good feeling that comes from spending time thinking about someone else's needs. The idea is for the adults and kids in the group to learn about each other and go home and practice being appreciative by doing something to take care of the needs of someone else in their family at least once a day.

KINDNESS IS CONTAGIOUS

Pretty much every morning, my wife will wake up and turn on the television. At 7 a.m., we'll get our daily dose of "All That Matters" in our world in 90 seconds. We watch a series of short clips showing scenes from around the world. I guess every day is a little different, but after a while, it all seems the same. We'll watch stories of natural disasters; school shootings; war; financial news; and the latest in the world of politics, entertainment, and sports. There's so much coming at us that it can be overwhelming, discouraging, or even flat-out depressing. Which is probably why the news always has some little "blooper" or "good neighbor" story.

Now before you get the idea that I'm just bashing the news, I want you to understand that's not my point. The way I see it, watching the news is like going to a buffet. When you go to a buffet, you have a lot to choose from. Some of it is kind of tasty, some of it is lousy, and it does get a little predictable at times. You make your choices, and if you choose wisely, you'll feel energized and well.

The same is true for the news. There will be a "buffet" of images that you can choose to select. Some stories will be scary, some sad, some funny, and some will make you think. These are the stories that will inspire you to go out and *do something*. In some ways, without really preaching at us, news can be a real call to action. The question is, what kind of action are you being called to? And then there is the related question, what kind of actions are your children being called to when they watch TV or take in the buffet from their Facebook feeds and elsewhere?

Depending on what your child watches, TV can be little more than a brain binky, which can be welcome relief at the end of the day. But TV and media in general can also be a way to teach our children about what it might feel like to follow their moral compass. Every day of every week, there are stories about real-life heroes, using their energy in amazing displays of kindness. We see the quick image of the firefighter, holding a baby, coming out of a burning building that could have killed them both. We see the image of the passerby who stepped in to stop some random act of violence. We see rescue workers entering into devastated areas, knowing they risk injury and infectious disease as they provide encouragement, food, and shelter for flood victims. Some call that courage; I call it kindness in its most dramatic form.

In the last lesson, we talked about the importance of children following their moral compass and how this helps build a sense of confidence. In our society, values like appreciation, generosity, and kindness are part of our national core standards. Kids who are encouraged to develop a habit of appreciation grow in confidence. So do kids who are encouraged to develop a habit of kindness. That's what I want to focus on in this lesson: how to build confidence by developing the habit of kindness in your child.

BAD NEWS AND GOOD NEWS CAN INSPIRE ACTS OF KINDNESS

For most of us, the urge to do something kind often gets kindled when we see or hear the news, or when the news comes to you. But kids with attention-deficit/hyperactivity disorder (ADHD) don't spend much time watching the news. Even when they do, or when they learn about a tragedy, their tendency to be easily distracted can get in the way of their focusing on the problems of others. Many children and adults have difficulty being compassionate, but it can be even harder if you happen to be someone with ADHD because forgetfulness and distractibility can get in the way. By the same token, if children with ADHD do lock onto the needs of others, their ability to hyperfocus on what they consider important can become a major source of change!

I live in an area where the "news has come to us" on several occasions. We've had two major floods in our area. One hit on my youngest sons' first day of school. Imagine being a parent, sending your children off to kindergarten with all sorts of reassurances like "You're going to have a great day today at school. Love you. See you after school." I was holding a video camera in one hand and an umbrella in the other as I recorded this precious moment.

By midday, the rain was coming down in sheets, huge puddles were starting to build up on the streets, and parents were getting calls that school was getting out early. The rain was so intense that some of the buses couldn't get through to bring the kids home safely, and some parents couldn't get to the school to reach their kids.

Helping networks were quickly formed. Parents teamed up with neighbors and schools and found a way to reach kids and keep them safe until they could get home. After the rains stopped, people worked together pumping floodwater from each other's homes and sharing whatever food and supplies we had. Kids got involved in the work, and some of them even organized toy deliveries to children who had lost their playthings. Hour after hour, day after day, week after week, kind acts like this are happening everywhere.

Because the news calls all of us to action, people from around the country came pouring in to help and bring in much-needed supplies. People in our community really appreciated the help. One truth came through loud and clear: The right thing to do was to be kind and to help. I have no doubt that everyone who pitched in felt the warmth and good feeling that comes from taking the time to "do what's right" by showing kindness. That's what we need to help our kids experience.

Calls to action don't necessarily have to come from bad news. They can come from some of those good news stories, too. One of my favorite good news stories came from something that happened at my church. A young man named Skip always wanted to go on a vacation to one of those warm, tropical islands in the winter. For years, he saved and saved and eventually was able to save up enough money to go on his dream vacation. Then something happened to Skip. As he thought about spending his money lounging on a beach, sipping cool drinks, and watching the waves come in and out in some version of paradise, he started feeling a passion to do something else with his money.

So instead of using the money to pay for his dream vacation, Skip decided to take his money and feed people. He donated all of it to buy the chicken needed to feed somewhere around 700 people in need of a good meal. When people at my church found out about it, we were all in. People donated money, restaurant owners donated their kitchens, volunteers came out to prepare and deliver food to our launching site on a street corner in one of the poorest sections of Binghamton on one of the coldest days in February just to hand out delicious chicken dinners to whoever walked by.

My kids were there as part of this experience of being kind, watching and helping out wherever they could. Life lessons like this about kindness will help my children and your children grow and live lives that matter, that make a difference.

In this lesson, I'd like you to continue to think about how you're trying to kindle a sense of doing something kind in your child. In the previous lesson, we talked about showing appreciation and how good it feels to do that. In this lesson, we're going to concentrate on encouraging kids to discover how good it feels to think about the needs of someone else and to do something to take care of others, rather than ourselves.

FROM SURVIVING TO SHARING

When I first started talking about kindness with my youngest sons, they were puzzled. The idea of thinking about what their brother would need or want rather than what they wanted or needed was a mindblower. Life has been some version of *Survivor*—a struggle to "outwit, outplay and out last" the other to win whatever it was that they were competing for. Getting every thing "I" want is Job 1. Everything else is a distant Number 2.

During the past 4 years, we've spent a lot of time helping our sons experiment with the idea of being kind, sharing, and caring about someone else. One of my favorite stories I've shared is the LEGO® blocks story. One day, I was in the kitchen, and a battle broke out between my little guys. Apparently there was a particular LEGO piece that both boys wanted. In the grabbing and tugging, one of the boys got hit by an elbow and was crying.

When I heard what happened, my initial urge was to say, "That's it, you can't play LEGOs for the rest of the day." Then it hit me. My boys were being selfish and not kind, so it was time for some Positive Practice. In my living room (we call it the LEGO room), there is a big bin of LEGO parts. I calmly gave the boys two large spaghetti pots and sat them on the floor. I took the bin of LEGO parts and calmly poured them onto the floor. I told my boys, "Guys, you just found out what happens when you're acting selfish. Now let's try something different. I want you to take turns looking over the LEGO pile and pick out one LEGO that you think your brother might like. Ask him if he'd like it, and if he does, give it to him. Then it will be your brother's turn to do the same for you." My sons looked down at the pile of more than a thousand LEGO pieces. I continued: "And I want you to do that for each other until the pile is done. You need to work on being more kind and less selfish."

So my sons started picking up one piece at a time, sharing it with each other. At first, they worked pretty slowly, carefully judging each piece they'd offer. After a little while, it must have dawned on them that they'd be there forever, so they asked permission to share by the handful. My hope was that they were realizing that the stuff they treasured so much really didn't matter. Hearing their gleeful laughter as they finished up sharing the pile was so much nicer than the squabbling over that treasured piece.

My sons' LEGO experience was the beginning of working on kindness at home. As they played games against each other, instead of winning at all costs and gloating about their good win feeling, I'd have each compliment his brother on any good move or play his brother made. When they came in the house after school, I taught them to say some version of "Hi, Mom, how's your day? Anything I can do to help out?" If I was doing some kind of chore, I looked for my sons to volunteer to help me without being asked. These are all acts of kindness, moments when you are aware of the needs of someone else and take care of them rather than yourself. And because of how human beings are built, that feels good and right.

Along the way, we needed to use motivational techniques such as Time Stands Still, Positive Practice, and Positive Punishment, and so will you (see Lesson 1 for a review of these techniques). Like I've said before, kids need a reason to learn any new skill, and it's unlikely that simply telling them you want them to be kind will turn things around. So be glad when your children are kind and help them to practice "the right stuff" when they're not. Gradually, kindness will begin to grow in your home.

TIPS FOR TEACHING KIDS TO BE KIND

Now it's your turn. If you haven't spent much time focusing your energy on helping your child learn about the importance of kindness, this is a good time to start. A good place to begin is to think about what's been happening where you live and then start to brainstorm about projects your child could work on with your family or a team of other kids and parents.

Over the years, I've been amazed at what kids can do. Some have organized toy donation programs for local shelters for homeless families. Some have started donation programs for abandoned dogs and cats. Some have volunteered at local "summer fun" programs for little kids. Some have run car washes or offered lawn care or other services and donated the money to a local charity. Some have decided to take part of their allowance, pool their money together, and sponsor a child through a program like Compassion International. There's no telling what your child might decide to do. Although getting together and having fun with other kids is a great way to build friendships, working on a project together with friends and family really bonds people together. Here's a worksheet you can use to get started.

Worksheet for Life Lesson 10: Kindness Is Contagious

Doing what you believe is right makes you feel good about yourself and helps you build confidence. This holds true when it comes to showing appreciation and for other values, like being generous, being tolerant, and being kind. When you do what you believe is right, you just feel better. That's how we're built.

Kindness can be shown in a variety of ways. It's not always national news stuff. It's seeing some kid in school, sitting alone at the cafeteria, and you walk over, sit down, and share a lunch. It's saying "Hey" at school to the kids who aren't high on the popularity scale. It's taking time to play with your little brother or sister instead of "doing what you want." It's stunning your mom or dad by taking a little of the burden off their shoulders and doing the dishes without being asked. It's noticing that your elderly neighbors' lawn is turning into a jungle and mowing it for them, and you don't ask for a dime.

It's also about kind acts outside your home. Bad stuff happens in every neighborhood or community sometimes. The kids who get involved in making things better end up feeling better and growing in confidence. So take a couple of minutes and think about what you've seen or heard about. First, team up with your parent or grandparent and answer these yes-or-no questions:

This week, did you hear about

- someone's house catching fire? _____
- someone getting killed in a car accident? _____
- someone's mother or father getting killed or wounded in war? _____
- a flood, tornado, or storm killing others and destroying homes? _____
- a village where people have no food or water? _____
- a child with a serious illness whose family needs help to pay for care? _____
- any other kind of situation in which people needed help? _____

Worksheet for Life Lesson 10: Kindness Is Contagious (*Continued*)

Of all the stories you heard about, which one drew you in and made you want to do something about it? Why?

_____

_____

_____

Now take some time and think about what you could do. By yourself or with your family or class, decide on one situation that you can help make better. What will you do to show kindness in that situation? Write about it here:

_____

_____

_____

Now that you've picked one situation to help, decide when you're going to put the first part of your plan into action. Do you need to meet with your group or a resource person to work on this together? When will you meet? Write down the first part of your plan here:

_____

_____

_____

A game might be a fun to conclude this lesson and change things up a bit. I usually go with an individual challenge. I might crumple pieces of paper into balls and see how many a child can toss into a wastebasket in 60 seconds. I might use a mini indoor basketball hoop hung on a doorframe and do the same thing. If you are doing this lesson at home, challenge your child to a game of indoor (or outdoor) hoops or some other game. The winner buys an ice cream for the loser. If you are doing this lesson with a group of kids, we ask the child who wins to do something different: Instead of keeping the prize, the child gives it to someone else. The child could decide to give it to someone in his or her life skills class. Or the child could give it to someone in need or a group that cares for people in need. The idea is to continue to practice being kind and experience how that feels.

ORGANIZATION IS NOT A FOUR-LETTER WORD!

Probably the most common problem for children with attention-deficit/hyperactivity disorder (ADHD) is their disorganization and tendency to get distracted when they are attempting to complete a task. You ask your kid to go and clean his room. This, I believe, is a universal request. If there is life on other planets, some alien kid on some distant planet is being told to clean up his room. And the alien kid is showing the same lack of immediate response that you have seen in your home. After reminding your child, repeatedly, the child does go to her room. To you, it's an overwhelming mess. To our kids, it's their little nest, complete with all their prized and precious toys, homework papers, snack wrappers, half-filled juice or soda bottles, cups, paper plates with dried-out bits of food, games, books, sports stuff, clothes they're always asking you to help them find, smelly socks that have been on the floor so long they're stiff, and sneakers, along with maybe several hundred LEGO® blocks strewn exactly the way they should be. And you've asked them to disturb their little bit of paradise.

Even if the child is inclined to get started on this monumental task, he usually has no idea where to begin. After all, everything is just where he left it, which is absolutely perfect! Now you might decide to help your kid get started on this task and direct him to begin by picking up his clothes and putting them away. You might even get specific and say, "Clean clothes are supposed to be in a drawer or hung up in the closet, and dirty clothes go in this basket." OK, that's pretty clear. But you know what's going to happen. On the way to picking up his socks, he notices some LEGO piece that he's been searching for. So he heads over to the LEGO collection. When you return in 30 minutes, your child is busily constructing some new flying thing. And he's also slurping on yet another drink pouch, and there's a bag of freshly opened Cheetos on the floor.

Now, if you happen to be an adult with ADHD (or are simply an exhausted, overworked parent), it's pretty likely that you do your version of the same thing. You start to pick up the family room and find an old bill that needs to be paid. So you pick it up and go to put it in the bill pile in the kitchen. On your way, you start feel a little hungry. Open the refrigerator, grab some milk. Go to the cabinet. Get some cereal. As you start to munch, you decide to turn on the TV. HGTV is showing the latest edition of *Love It or List It*. As the program ends, there's an invitation to enter some kind of contest to win your dream home. You head for the computer, leaving the box of cereal, bill, and milk carton on the table. "You've Got Mail" invites you to check your e-mail. In a click, you're busy checking e-mail, which reminds you that you haven't caught up with your Facebook friends in a while. A text message comes in. You text back. You forget to enter the contest, check e-mail or Facebook, or put the cereal and milk away, much less what you started to do in the first place (remember that bill on the floor in the family room?). Frustrating, isn't it? It's not surprising that your child will get distracted too and get lost on the way to doing what you asked.

So what do you do? Yelling might come to mind, but that's going to get you nowhere. You could patiently remind your child over and over again to get started. But honestly, you're only going to get frustrated when he still doesn't clean up, so you'll end up yelling anyway. *You* might get distracted, forget, and later realize your child didn't organize his room, and get mad then. You could punish him by taking away his stuff or grounding him. Chances are, by the time he's finished griping, whining, yelling, or screaming at you, you'll regret that you bothered to ask him to clean up in the first place. The bottom line is that until you take the time to teach your kids, guide them, and practice with them, they're not going to learn how to organize their possessions.

The same is true about other kinds of organizational tasks because getting organized isn't just about "stuff." Kids need to learn how to organize and keep track of their assignments so that they don't forget their homework. They need to keep track of their activity schedule so that they don't forget to pack their stuff for basketball practice. They also need to learn how to plan their time to achieve goals that are important to them. As kids set goals, plan out the various in-between steps that need to be taken to complete the task, and set prompts and reminders to keep them on task and on schedule, they begin to feel the sense of accomplishment and grow in confidence from taking on and completing a project. So, in this lesson, we talk about organizing your kids' schedule, helping them achieve their goals, and working on "organizing stuff."

GET YOUR GAME FACE ON: IT'S TIME TO SORT AND CONQUER THE STUFF

To get started teaching this, you'll need to work with your child to get her room in order. Right now, your child has no clue what an organized room looks like. That will be something that you'll need to help her see. So my first question for you is: What do you want your child's room to look like? Where do you want her to put clothes, shoes, books, papers, toys, and food and drink debris? Once you have that in mind, you're ready to answer my second question: When do you want the room to look like the picture in your mind? Every morning? Every night before your children have dinner? On Saturday morning before they go off to play? Whenever you get mad enough to make an issue out of it?

I've found that in the beginning, getting things squared away every day is a good way to start. As a kid, my mom would do "room check" every morning before we went to school. If the bed wasn't made to her liking, if there were clothes anywhere they shouldn't be, if there were books, toys, papers, or food and drink debris to be found at room-check time (before we went downstairs to eat breakfast), we'd have to clean it either before school (if we had time) or when we got home. And because we hadn't done it before room check, my mom did her version of Positive Punishment and Time Stands Still. We had to do some other chores after we got home and couldn't play anything until we did these extra chores.

Using those kinds of strategies to motivate your child will be helpful once you've established a certain standard and your child has made the initial effort, but Step 1 of that first pass is all about "staging" the room. When you decide that it's time for you to teach your child how to organize his stuff, pick a day for "room cleanup." You're going to need to dedicate the time and energy to get it looking just the way you'd like, because your child has no clue—and even if he did, he'd get distracted and never get the job done.

It doesn't matter what you start with; it could be clothes, toys, books, papers—whatever. It's probably best to work out of piles and bags. Put all the clothes in a pile and all the obvious trash in a garbage bag. Books would go in one pile, school papers in another. Toys in another spot, plates and food or drink stuff somewhere else. In time, you'll start to see the floor again!

Now that you have everything in piles, it's time to decide what's going to stay in the room and what's getting tossed out. There are a variety of rules for deciding what should stay in a room and what should go. The simplest one I know is that if you haven't used something in a year, it probably isn't essential to keep in your room. The first pile to take on is the easiest one: It's the one with trash, old food, drink pouches and bottles, bowls, plates, and other discard items. That's a job that's easily dispatched by taking a plastic bag or two to the garage (or wherever you put trash) and returning bowls, plates, and flatware to the kitchen.

Next, take on the clothes. Every item of clothing will need a home, and you'll need to be clear on what goes where. Socks need a home; underwear needs a home; and so do shorts, jeans, sweatshirts, school clothes, and uniforms. If you need to use labels to mark what drawer is for what, fine. What's important is that the child begins to realize that everything has a home in her room. As you're sorting through the clothes pile, you'll usually find a number of articles that your child no longer wears. Put them in a bag or box and get them out of her room. They can be given to another family member, a neighbor, donated to a charity, or sold at a garage sale.

Next, take on the books. Any book that your child still enjoys reading will need a home in her room or somewhere else in the home where books are stored. Any book that she doesn't read anymore needs to be moved out of the room and placed in a bag or box to donate to a library, school, or some other place where kids read books.

Finally, take on the pile of toys. Again, every toy needs a home. However, unlike clothes and books, many kids have too many toys to fit in their bedroom. So just like with the other stuff, a toy that hasn't been played with for a year could bring some joy to another kid. It could be given to a brother or sister. It could be shared with another kid in the neighborhood, donated, or sold at a garage sale. In fact, one of the ways my wife and I have inspired our children to clean out their rooms is to let them sell old books, clothes, and toys at our yearly garage sale. We ask them to donate 10% of what they make to charity, save 10%, and spend the rest on something they like. Over the years, my boys have become pretty shrewd negotiators. This year, they made $81 at their very own garage sale!

When you begin this organization day, remember the importance of completing the job on the day you start. The deal is that the work must get done so that the room is looking the way you'd like *before your child goes to bed that night.* Try to make it fun. My dad was great at getting me into variations of basketball games in which I'd shoot trash into cans, clothes into baskets, and so on. I'm guessing that you'll be able to do the same.

ORGANIZING SCHOOL PAPERS

I usually save this job for last. Once clothes, toys, trash, and food stuff are put away, it's time to turn your child's attention to school papers. I've always been amazed at how many math and science worksheets, art treasures, poems and other creative writing papers end up somewhere in our homes. During the school year, some of this stuff is actually important to hang on to, particularly worksheets, study guides, and other papers that may make it easier to pass those "common core standard" tests at the end of the year. After a couple of decades of fatherhood, not to mention working with a few thousand kids in my practice, I've come up with a strategy that seems to work pretty well.

> Step 1: Sort out the papers into subject areas. Then make a decision about whether any of the papers will be helpful when it comes to taking those end-of-the-year exams. If so, put them into a folder that will get stored when your child is done sorting. If not, they're headed for the recycling bin.
> Step 2: Teach your child how to keep a filing system. Each subject folder needs to be easily identified and placed into either

a filing cabinet or one of those heavy cardboard boxes that you can pick up pretty inexpensively at one of the "big box" stores. For my patients, the ideal desk is an old door or piece of plywood (let them paint it any way they want) that rests on top of a couple of two- or three-drawer file cabinets. Gives kids a lot of space for their writing assignments and (if they're fortunate enough) for their computer and printer, and more than enough space for their papers.

FOLLOW THROUGH WITH THE ROOM CHECK

Once the room is the way you like and school papers are filed away, set up your version of daily room-check time. No matter when that time is, you've got to follow through, make sure the room is looking good before your child has the "OK to play." As with the other lessons I've taught, Positive Practice, Positive Punishment, and Time Stands Still are very helpful in keeping children motivated to keep their room looking good. As children get older, they'll want more input into how the room is organized. This is fine as long as they develop a way to keep their stuff organized that is acceptable to you.

ORGANIZING TIME

Students with ADHD really have difficulty organizing their time. When they were little kids, other people made sure that they turned in all their forms on time. Their teacher made sure that they wrote down their homework assignments. Their parents checked to make sure when their assignments were due. Mom and Dad nagged them to break down long-term projects into doable parts. Someone else would keep track of the family calendar and write down practice schedules, school activity schedules, doctor's appointments, and so on. As they get older, children with ADHD have to learn how to organize their time; otherwise, they will not succeed in college.

Failure to succeed during the first year of college is one of the most common reasons older teens and young adults are referred to my clinic for evaluation and treatment. High school graduates with ADHD who are heading out to college are at high risk for academic probation by the end of the first semester and asked to leave their college after the end of the second semester. How does this happen? Here's a version of the story I hear time and time again.

"Tommy" was a student who was always considered to be "a really smart kid." He was incredibly good at certain subjects (often science or math, sometimes social studies, rarely English). Many of his teachers would comment that his grades would be better if only he'd do his homework. They'd encourage him to use a planner to keep track of assignments, but nothing much happened. During middle school and high school, Tommy's grades were typically about 15 to 20 points below what they should have been.

Instead of being a high-80 to mid-90 student, Tommy was more of a high-60 to low-80 student, except for those subjects he loved. He failed to complete several homework assignments every week, delayed beginning his papers, and occasionally didn't turn in papers and projects on time. His parents nagged him and reminded him to get his homework done, but it was the same story year after year: Test grades were typically high, homework grades were typically low. Net out: Tommy was a high C, low B student.

After graduating from high school, some students like Tommy attend a community college. Their parents insist that they stay local so that they can develop better study habits. Others convince their parents that they'll do so much better at an expensive private college or university. Unfortunately, the story is often the same, regardless of the college they choose. At first, Tommy will go to class but not do any work after he leaves the lecture hall. After all, there aren't too many college classes where the professor gives daily assignments and checks them. Instead, their professors will provide him with the course syllabus, listing the content of classes, the dates of exams, and when term papers are due.

Unfortunately, because the professor doesn't require that anything be done on a daily basis, students with ADHD drift through the first several months at school. They develop friendships, have fun, and enjoy their newfound freedom. But because they haven't learned to complete reading assignments on a daily basis and how to break down writing assignments into small daily or weekly steps, maybe they'll go to class, but chances are they'll do nothing until deadline time.

This strategy might have worked during high school, but it's not going to be a winning idea at the college level. Unlike high school, there's no one who's going to send an e-mail to Mom or Dad letting them know that Tommy didn't go to class. Nobody's going to let Mom or Dad know that Tommy didn't turn in his midterm paper and failed his first exam. But Tommy will know, which may make him anxious or depressed, or it may simply lead him to engage in some wishful thinking: "It's OK, I've got plenty of time to make up for that grade."

So Tommy starts missing more classes. His parents will call and ask him how it's going, and it's always "Fine." The first semester comes to a close, and Tommy has no idea how he's done . . . but he's thinking it's not good. Somehow his professors never file their grades, and his parents (who have no access to his academic status because their son is no longer a minor) wait and hope. Then the bad news hits. Tommy gets the letter from the dean of his college or university informing him that he's on academic probation and must meet with the university to set up some kind of plan. By this point, he's got a GPA of 1.25 and needs to raise it to a 2.0 or he's out. Now he's got to be a solid B student at the college level (something he's never done before) or he's out of luck. Despite panicked parent and college attempts at intervention, most of these kids will end up flunking out of their first college.

I'm hoping that this story doesn't seem too far-fetched to you. It's a part of the daily reality at my Attention Disorders Clinic. My perspective is that children who don't figure out time management skills will really struggle in their efforts to transition into college and adulthood. Without learning time management skills, kids like Tommy aren't going anywhere.

HOW TO STOP BEING YOUR CHILD'S BRAIN

Even though Tommy's story might be discouraging, the truth is that organizational and time management skills can be learned at any age. However, we all have to wrap our heads around one truth: Tommy's difficulty in organizing, planning, and completing tasks is founded on neurological problems, not motivational ones. Sure, it would be great if Tommy were motivated to learn how to get organized, and we'll talk about how to motivate kids with ADHD to learn organizational skills. But it's just as important to realize that the brain structures that are involved in helping us get organized (like the frontal lobes and the cerebellum) need to be activated too. Tommy went through life without his frontal lobes and cerebellum ever learning how to do this.

Have you ever wondered about your child's ability to estimate time? Here are a couple of challenges you could give her to check this out. Ask her to estimate the number of steps it would take to go from the place where she is to a place in the visible distance. Then ask her to tell you how long it would take for her to get there. Then ask her to measure the distance in steps and time. Chances are she won't even come close. I hope you can understand that if your child can't even estimate the number of steps and amount of time it would take simply to get from the kitchen to her bedroom, then she is really going to have a hard time figuring out how long it would take to finish a reading, writing, or math assignment. Without repeated practice, the brain regions that take care of these jobs won't develop. And the little boy who can't get out the door for the school bus without mom nagging will become the college student who doesn't make it to class on time.

To learn how to get better at estimating time and the number of steps it takes to accomplish any task will take instruction, practice, and parent reinforcement to make sure that the child practices and learns. Of all the life lessons that we've covered, the development of organizational skills is one of the hardest to learn—and the one most likely to be ignored by parents. The truth is, we just get worn out and give up believing that our kids can ever organize themselves. We become our children's frontal lobes and cerebellum and take care of the organization and time management tasks for them. We'll text them throughout the day to remind them about their responsibilities. We keep their personal schedule of activities for them. We pack their lacrosse bags. We wash their clothes and make sure their uniforms are clean. We find their missing spikes, gloves, papers, books, and book bag. The list of what we do is endless. And all the while, the parts of their brain that need to be developing lie dormant.

Let's go back to the story of Tommy. From my perspective, Tommy should never head off to any college without the following being established: First, if Tommy wants someone else to pay for his tuition, that someone else better have permission to contact whomever they need to at the school to make sure that Tommy is attending class, meeting with academic advisors or tutors, learning how to organize and complete work, and getting assignments turned in on time. This is because the senior in high school who is not organizing and completing assignments will not become a college freshman who is organized and on top of things without help. It's also important for you to realize that if Tommy is going to succeed at college, he'll need to become involved in tutoring and academic coaching programs that are available at many college learning centers. And before you send in any tuition money, you need to make sure that Tommy has given written permission for you to be in communication with his academic advisor, tutors, and professors.

When your child was in grades K to 12, the Family Educational Rights and Privacy Act (FERPA) gave you the right to inspect and review his or her educational records. Once our children reach age 18 or become a student at any type of educational program after high school, they, too, have the right to this type of information. However, it is important for you to realize that this does not mean you lose your right. FERPA allows a college or university to share educational information with a parent with or without a student's consent if the student is claimed as a dependent on your income tax return (or in situations in which the health of the student is at risk or the student has violated the law or university policy regarding the use of alcohol or a controlled substance). Even with this waiver, I encourage parents to make life simpler and require your son or daughter to sign a waiver permitting your access to their educational records before they head off to college. Sometimes, knowing that your parents can check on things like class attendance, completion of work, and performance on exams can help a student make better choices during the early days of college.

Second, Tommy needs to know that there is a clear cutoff date for withdrawal from classes without financial penalty. If he is not fulfilling his responsibilities, the person(s) paying for college will withdraw him from the college or university. Period. I'm figuring that most of you don't have $20,000 to throw away for your son or daughter to have a nice 2-month vacation in a place called college. If your child does not have the neurological foundation to succeed (i.e., is not receiving effective treatment for his ADHD) or is not sufficiently motivated to seek out the necessary tutorial support, college is not the place to be. However, if your "Tommy" is being treated effectively for ADHD and has established a working relationship with academic advisors, coaches, and tutors, then college will be a great place for him to develop abilities and grow into an effective adult.

WHAT CAN I DO NOW, EVEN IF COLLEGE IS STILL A FEW YEARS AWAY?

Now's a good time to begin to work on organization of time, regardless of your child's age. Time management has four general components:

1. determining what needs to be done,
2. figuring out how long the task will take,
3. deciding when the task will be started, and
4. setting a foolproof prompt to get you started.

Depending on the child's age, you may end up using non-electronic tools such as dry marker boards, chalkboards, a desk calendar, or an appointment book, or you may find that electronic tools such as a phone, tablet, or a computer are best to keep your family on top of things.

DETERMINING WHAT NEEDS TO BE DONE

A lot of the young children I work with do well with a big dry marker board placed on the wall in their bedroom. This type of board is great for writing down what needs to be done. A good way to begin is to decide on the tasks that need to be planned and completed for the morning, afternoon, and evening. That's a good topic to cover in one of your weekly family meetings. Include on the list of tasks ones that are important to your child as well as ones that are important to you.

ESTABLISHING START-UP TIMES AND PROMPTS

Just like organizing stuff, we all need to figure out when we are going to start a task, how long it will take, and what will prompt us to start. Your child will need to practice these skills too. If she needs to pick up her room, there needs to be a decision made as to when this task will be started. If she needs to work on homework, there needs to be a decision made as to when it will be started. And this decision needs to consider how long it's likely to take to finish the job. Just as important, you'll need to set a foolproof prompt. Younger kids will probably use some version of a written chart. Older kids, who might have access to a phone, tablet, or computer, could do the same with their electronic device.

I've provided a sample chart that you might use. It includes the task, the planned start-up time, the prompt that will be used, the child's guesses about when he or she will start and finish, and the actual time completed. Just like any charting system, feel free to assign points for success and give some type of reward. However, if the child does not do the task as planned, then he or she will need to do some kind of Positive Practice (like setting a time to do another task during the day and making that happen on time) and doing something to make up for missing the target (Positive Punishment). As always, your child does not have your OK to do anything else until the Positive Practice and make-up task (Time Stands Still) have been completed.

The use of Positive Practice, Positive Punishment, and Time Stands Still is not meant to be "mean." It's simply a way of reinforcing the notion that in life, if we don't do what we promise to do (or are supposed to do), we need to do the right thing and do something to make up for not keeping our word. It's not OK to go on with our life until we do. That's true for adults, and that's true for kids.

My To-Do List

Stuff I've Got to Do	I Will Start At	My Reminder Prompt	I Think I'll Finish at	I Actually Started at	I Actually Finished at

Let's take a simple example, tooth brushing. Say that you and your children decided it was time for them to take responsibility for brushing their teeth in the morning without you nagging them. During your family meeting, your children list "brush my teeth" on their chart, and together you figure out when tooth brushing needs to be done. Then your children will need to figure out what prompt they'll use. They might say that when their favorite TV show is done, they'll head off and brush their teeth. They might set a timer in the kitchen to go off every day at "teeth-brushing" time. They might set an alarm on their watch or phone or use an app like Choicework that can remind them when it's time to do a wide range of tasks. To make it a bit more fun, we can ask our children to predict when they're going to start and when they'll finish.

Lots of people have invested all sorts of money into a variety of electronic timers and prompting devices, which is fine. I've listed some of those at the end of this lesson. Use whatever you and your child think might work. Sometimes you'll hit on a winning prompt the first time. Other times, you might have to try out a couple of ideas before something works. Even though this may seem a little tedious, realize that if you don't get your kids working on using their brain to remember their schedules, they are not getting trained to do a task that will make all the difference when they attempt to launch into adulthood.

Just as important as deciding on a task and setting a prompt is deciding on some type of motivator to inspire children to do what they set out to do. Without a compelling reason to do something, learning isn't likely. That's where strategies such as Positive Practice, Positive Punishment, and Time Stands Still come in. Let's say that a child decides that he is going to brush his teeth after a particular show comes on in the morning. Or that he's going set a timer and do it then. But he doesn't; he forgets or "whatever" happens.

Because his strategy didn't work out, when he comes home after school, he'll need to practice brushing his teeth before he does anything else (Positive Practice). Then he'll need to do something to motivate himself to remember to do it tomorrow, like having to read about what kinds of things can happen if he doesn't brush his teeth and then writing a list of five of those problems. Because he caused frustration by not keeping his word to you, he will need to do something to help you feel a little better, like helping you fix dinner, sing, play a musical instrument, or whatever would help you (Positive Punishment). After he does these things, he can get on with his life (Time Stands Still). During this time, your child could also talk with you about another prompt he could use that might work better.

Let's take on another example. How about the child who decides that it's time for her to take responsibility for getting her homework done and turned in? OK, first, the child has to figure out a way to record her assignments and bring home the necessary materials. Then she has to pick a time to start her homework, estimating out how long it will take. She'll need some kind of prompts to remember to write down her assignments and some kind of prompt to start doing the work. Finally, she has to get it done.

If the child is successful, great! If not, then you and your child will need to see where the plan fell apart. Did she not get homework done because she didn't record it somewhere? OK, then she'll need to decide whether her strategy to record homework was a good one or if she wants to change it. Did she not get her homework done because she didn't know how to do it or got distracted because she tried to work for too long? OK. If that's the case, then you and your child will need to figure out how to take care of these problems.

More often, our kids will not get their homework done because they got home, ignored whatever prompt they set, and ended up watching TV, playing a computer game, or visiting with their friends. If that's the case, then you and your child will have to reach a decision about access to these activities before her work is done.

Whatever the reason is that she didn't complete her work, your child will still need to complete that assignment (plus another one that you'll create) before she can do anything fun. If she says she "lost" the assignment or her teacher won't accept late assignments, that's OK. The lesson remains, "If you don't take care of your responsibilities, you'll still have to do the task (or an equivalent amount of work) plus a penalty." I'll often use basketball, hockey, soccer, or other sports as an example. In these games, a "penalty" shot is awarded if a player breaks the rules. In the game of school, not doing homework is against the rules, and a penalty assignment will be given. For science, history, and reading, just head to Wikipedia or another resource, pick out a topic, ask the child to find out certain information and write it down for you. For math, there are a number of websites that can be used to help your child practice math at any grade (e.g., http://www.ixl.com; http://www.xtramath.com). When she has completed these penalty tasks, she can start having fun.

Just like learning to brush teeth, completing homework gets the child's brain into planning mode and exercises the frontal lobes and cerebellum. The same is true for daily room cleaning, washing athletic clothes for games, and keeping daily and weekly activity schedules. Every day a child works on taking responsibility for planning and completing a chore or task, these regions of the brain are developing, setting the stage for a smoother transition into college life and beyond.

MAKING DREAMS HAPPEN

Getting organized does not just mean finding a way to complete all our chores and responsibilities. It also has to do with making our dreams happen. One of the most fun parts of leading life skills classes is helping kids think about what they'd like to make happen in their lives. In the "believe it or not" category, here are a couple of examples of what kids have done. I had one child who dreamed about going to a Boston Red Sox baseball game. To do this, he'd have to be able to pay for a ticket for himself and his dad and gas to the game and back from Binghamton, New York. His parents could not afford such a trip. Total cost for the day was estimated to be about $200. So my patient started to mow lawns, do yard work, and collect bottles and cans, and by the end of the season, he was able to treat himself and his dad to great day at Fenway Park.

Another one of my students was even more ambitious. His dream was to go to Disney World. It was the beginning of fall, and he had a lot of work ahead of him if he was going to make it. His parents figured out the costs and agreed that if he could come up with enough money for his airfare and admission to the park, one of them would cover the room, food, and their own airfare and admission. So my patient went to work. Put little flyers on all of his neighbor's houses, handed some out at church, and offered to do yard work, snow shoveling, lawn mowing, pet sitting, and any other jobs a kid could do. By the end of the following summer, he had saved enough for the trip!

One last story: I'll never forget a teenage girl, whom I'll call Michelle, who had a dream of making her high school cheerleading squad. She had never cheered before. Michelle came up with the following plan. First, she needed to get good at somersaults, handstands, back flips, and other moves. So she enrolled in a gymnastics class and just focused on those activities.

Next, she figured it'd be a good idea to get familiar with the routines. Each year in my area, there are regional cheerleading competitions for football cheerleading and basketball cheerleading. At these events, students from all over my region put together some amazing routines and compete to see which squad is the best. Well, the year before she tried out for her team, Michelle purchased a copy of the DVD for each of these events and started working on the routine her school used.

The last part of her plan was to make herself known to the high school coach. She found out that the coach was part of a group of people who ran a cheerleading camp at a nearby university. So Michelle signed up for the camp. She learned a lot of helpful tips for making the squad and impressed her coach with her enthusiasm and determination. When she tried out for her high school team at the end of the summer, she made the team.

Maybe you think that these stories are made-up ways to make you believe you and your child can make amazing things happen. Maybe you think that other kids could do it, but not your child. I just want you to know that pretty much anyone who ever became successful got there after a whole bunch of disappointments. When we try something that doesn't work out, one of two things can happen. Either we give up, or we will find another way to get the job done. And if we persevere and are onto something that's a good idea, eventually we're going to succeed.

Not all kids have such dreams. And some kids have parents who figure out ways to make as many of their kids' dreams happen as possible without any effort on the part of their children. Although such parent actions may be loving, generous, kind, and thoughtful, they don't contribute to the development of a child's planning ability. Thus, this lesson is intended to encourage children to use their own frontal lobes and cerebellum to accomplish the goals they set for their lives.

TIPS FOR TEACHING ORGANIZATIONAL SKILLS

Teaching organizational skills covers numerous parts of a child's life. Feel free to use the worksheet at the end of this lesson to help you get organized. It covers the essentials of organization, including organizing stuff, responsibilities, and making dreams happen.

Because this lesson focuses on organization, you might find it helpful to sit with your child and talk about some of the other lessons that you've been teaching. It would be a good time to talk about your child's kindness project or encourage him in some of the other changes that he's beginning to make in his life. If you'd like to compare how your child is doing now with how he was doing when you first started teaching the lessons in this book, you can use the Functional Assessment Checklist form again (found in the Introduction to this book and online at http://pubs.apa.org/books/supp/monastra-teaching).

Just like with the other lessons, it's always fun to have a game at the end. I'll usually play a "stacking" kind of game when I teach the lesson with a group. You could do the same with your family. In this activity the players compete on a game that is meant to be a playful version of organizing "stuff." Set up a table and place a stack of 28 plastic 16-ounce cups on the table. Tell your child he or she has 1 minute to build a cup tower that has a base of seven cups (if you are working with a group of children, each child will take a 1-minute turn). The other rows of cups are to have six, five, four, three, two, and one cup. The child who builds the highest tower in 60 seconds (or the one who builds the tower of 28 cups in the fastest time) wins the prize. If you're playing this game at home, you can challenge your child to this game or divide the family into teams. The "losing" family member or team makes a meal, prepares a dessert, or does something else that the "winning" person or team can enjoy.

Worksheet for Life Lesson 11: Organization Is Not a Four-Letter Word

For a lot of kids, getting organized doesn't sound like much fun. How about you? When people say to you, "You need to get organized!" what do you think they mean? Let's start with that. Take a few minutes to jot down the first five things that come to your mind when someone says, "You need to get organized."

"Get organized" means:

_____

_____

_____

_____

_____

Did you write down putting away things like toys, clothes, paper, and books? That's pretty typical.

How about taking care of responsibilities, such as homework, practice times for sports, and other activities? Most kids think of that kind of stuff too.

How about your dreams or hopes or plans for things that you'd like to do that would be really fun, like going to a pro football game or an amusement park? Did you write down any of those kinds of things?

Part 1. Organizing My Stuff

Everything in your room needs to have a "home." That way you can find things when you need them. Talk with your parents or grandparents about where your books, clothes, toys, and food are supposed to go. What did you decide?

In my house, books go:

_____

_____

Clothes go:

_____

_____

Worksheet for Life Lesson 11: Organization Is Not a Four-Letter Word (*Continued*)

Toys go:

_____

_____

Food/dishes go:

_____

_____

OK, now that you have an idea of where everything needs to go, you'll need to decide when you're going to get things put away. You and your parents or grandparents will need to pick a day when you have the time to put your books, clothes, toys, and food stuff away. Once you have the room picked up for the first time, then you'll need to figure out the time each day when you need to move things back to their homes.

My family and I decided that we're going to pick up the place on _____ (date) at _____ (time). Once my room is picked up, then I've got to have everything where it's supposed to go by _____ (time) every day.

Part 2. Keeping My Schedule

Right now, who keeps you on schedule? Do you wake up in the morning by yourself, or do your parents or grandparents do this for you? Do you keep track of your morning routine so that you make the bus, or does someone else? Do you schedule your homework time, organize your bags for your sports or recreational activities, and arrange for a ride, or does someone else? The sooner you start doing this, the better.

So let's start now. If you're going to take over this schedule-keeping job, you're going to need a way to keep track of your activities and some kind of reminder other than Mom or Dad nagging at you. You can use a dry marker board or calendar on the wall or a planner calendar that sits on your desk. You can use an assignment sheet to jot down work and

(continued)

Worksheet for Life Lesson 11: Organization Is Not a Four-Letter Word (*Continued*)

other responsibilities. Or you can use the opportunity to "take over this job" as a way to finally get that tablet or smartphone you've been hoping for. Those kinds of devices will not only help you to keep track of your schedule but you can also use them to set an alarm and let you know that it's time to do something on your schedule. Talk with your parents or grandparents and decide what you'll use this week. Read this next sentence, decide how you're going to do it, and write it down.

I'm going to take over waking up, eating the right stuff, getting to school, recording my assignments, completing my homework, keeping track of my appointments and practice/game schedule, and getting to bed so I get a decent night's sleep. This week I'm going to use _____ _____ to make it happen.

Most people find that it takes some time and practice to change an old habit. Don't be surprised if you mess up from time to time. Just remember, the goal is for you to be in control of your stuff and your time, otherwise you'll just go back to letting your parents be your brain, reminding you of everything you need to do.

Part 3. Making Dreams Happen

Organization is more than putting your stuff away and making sure you take care of your responsibilities. Organization is how we make our dreams come true.

So what's your dream? What would you like to make happen? Take your time and pick out something that you'd really like to make happen.

My dream is to _____.

Sit with your parents and get that organizing, planning part of your brain working (in case you were curious, the frontal lobes and the cerebellum are in charge of these jobs). Break down reaching your dream into little steps and then get started. You might be able to work on it a bit tonight. Chances are, you'll need more time at home with your parents to work out the details. Use this form to write down your plan.

Here's what I'm going to make happen: _____

Worksheet for Life Lesson 11: Organization Is Not a Four-Letter Word (*Continued*)

Here's what I'm going to do to make it happen:

1. _____
2. _____
3. _____
4. _____
5. _____
6. _____

After you've got the steps down, begin to use your calendar, smartphone, tablet, or whatever you're using to keep track of your time to set prompts to help you get started. It's really important for you (and that amazing brain of yours) to start to realize that you can make dreams come true! Once you've got that idea going, there's no telling what you can make happen!

PERSISTENCE PAYS OFF

I don't know about you, but every time I take a class, it's hard for me to remember, much less put into action, all of the information that's been shared with me. An expert at Home Depot could give me the step-by-step plans to install a new garbage disposal complete with a manual and colored photos, and I'd still need to call some 800 number or watch the YouTube installation video. I once tried to surprise my wife and kids with a Rachael Ray "simple, easy, 30-minute meal." It ended up taking me 2½ hours, and at the end, it tasted so bad that we ended up ordering takeout.

If you've presented all the life lessons in this book, made a plan with your child to put each new skill into action, and even practiced with role-plays and real-life scenarios, don't be discouraged if your child hasn't learned all of the lessons, *yet*. If your child is like the vast majority of the kids who've been through our life skills program, chances are he or she is starting to show signs of maybe three or four lessons taking root. That would be typical for most of my patients.

When I've examined the kinds of skills that are developing early in the process, the vast majority of the kids in my program have made headway establishing better eating, sleeping, and exercise habits. Their parents have started to nag less, take away less, and use Positive Practice, Positive Punishment, and Time Stands Still a lot more often. Because of that, their children are beginning to be calmer, argue less, and whine less. I hope this is what you're starting to experience in your home.

SOME LESSONS WILL "TAKE" SOONER THAN OTHERS, AND THAT'S OK

The early development of some of the other life skills seems to be anchored on what has grabbed the attention of parents. After completing the first 11 life skills lessons, I've found that about 25% of the kids now have rooms that are organized, and their parents have daily room checks. About 25% are working on getting braver or getting good at something that matters to their peers. Kids who had no interest in any organized community activity are now joining sports or recreational programs and "sticking with it," often accompanied by another member of their life skills class. Kids that have always shied away from any involvement in school activities are now (with the help of their parents and school counselor or teacher) part of some kind of sports, musical, drama, or social club at school.

Most of the groups of kids are now working together and have started to do some kind of group "kindness" project. This has led to some pairing up of kids for some social get-togethers, particularly if their parents have found the beginnings of some new adult friendships. The majority of families have begun to have weekly family meetings. These are the families that seem to be making the most headway in teaching values and promoting kindness and appreciation in the home.

So if you're at a place where you're seeing change in about three or four skill areas, be encouraged! That's about par for the course. As for the other skills, realize that learning how to start and maintain interesting conversations, respond to teasing, show engaging facial expressions, and shift from a "me first" orientation to one of caring about others is harder to master and will take more time and experience. Like I said during the class, learning how to come up with something to say during any kind of conversation is really hard for my patients. It's probably the life skill that takes the longest to develop.

When you think about it, being able to have a conversation means that the child is listening, is able to quickly remember some kind of information that has something to do with what's being said, and can speak about the topic before the conversation shifts. That is just not a skill that's going to magically develop by your child sitting in class or at a lunch table. This will take time and systematic work. There are different kinds of working memory games, like Scattergories and Lumosity, that exercise the brain centers that help kids with these kinds of tasks. Speech therapists, who are familiar with developing pragmatic language skills, can also give you some exercises that you could try. If you've taken part in a skill class, use the connections you've made in the class to help your child practice these kinds of skills. Unless your child starts to practice these skills on a daily basis, they are not likely to develop conversational skills.

A SOCIAL NETWORK SUPPORTS YOUR CHILD AND YOU

From my perspective, the development of a social network that encourages the development of social skills is one of the big reasons I spent so much time developing the life skills program. Before I began my life skills classes, my patients simply had no social network. They'd go to school and not talk with anyone. After school, they'd come home and not talk with their parents. They'd grab a snack and head to the TV room or their bedroom and not say anything to anyone for hours. They wouldn't be involved in any type of activity with peers. These were the kids who by the time they were into their teenage years were entrenched in a lifestyle that was killing any chance that they'd grow in self-confidence and communication skills.

That doesn't have to happen to your child. If you're involved in a life skills group, you now have a small group of potential friends for your son or daughter. I have little doubt that someone else in the group will be responsive to the idea of getting the kids together to help the kids grow. Just like when your children were little and you arranged play dates, chances are you'll have to take the lead in contacting the parents of the other children to set up times when your families will get together. That way, you can help to model and guide your child in having conversations in a more natural setting.

If you have been working on these lessons on your own and are feeling a little discouraged, now might be a good time to connect with other parents of children or teens with ADHD. Your child's school psychologist, social worker, or guidance counselor might know of local support groups or be interested in helping you start such a group. Now that you have this guidebook to help you, share the information with counselors at school and see what they think.

Another way that people connect with others is through support groups like Children and Adults With ADHD (www.chadd. org). This organization also offers opportunities to network with other parents of children with ADHD at annual conferences and local support group.

IF IT SEEMS LIKE YOU ARE NOT MAKING PROGRESS . . .

The take-home message for you is that what matters most to you will be the most likely skill to develop. Whatever you take the time to systematically teach and reinforce through practice will start to change. If you persist, it will typically pay off. I've found that the most progress is made by parents who decide to meet once a week as a family to review how everyone is doing and decide what will be done to move things in the right direction. I've also learned that parents who have decided to stop with nagging and taking away and are now using Positive Practice, Positive Punishment, and Time Stands Still are also seeing better progress.

Even though persistence typically pays off, there are times when parents might not be seeing any change, despite their best efforts. When that is the case, there are usually several explanations. The most common is that the child has some kind of medical problem that's been missed along the way. Research conducted at our clinic and elsewhere has revealed that mood, conduct, and attention problems can be caused by conditions as simple as a vitamin D deficiency, hypoglycemia, diabetes, an ongoing sleep disorder, inadequate diet, or other conditions. As I've looked more closely at the frequency of such conditions in the children coming to our clinic, I've found that other medical problems occur in approximately 35% to 40% of my patients. An additional 20% to 25% of my patients have undiagnosed or untreated visual tracking and convergence disorders.

Until recently, screening for such conditions has not been part of routine medical practice. That has begun to change with the establishment of new guidelines for psychiatric care, which can be found in the fifth edition of the *Diagnostic and Statistical Manual of Mental Disorders*. This manual clearly states the rationale for conducting an evaluation of these kinds of problems. So if your child is not making the kind of progress that I've described, checking into these kinds of problems is a good idea.

Another idea worth considering is that the child's medication is not the right one for them or that the dose is not effective. In my research, I've reported that there appear to be two neurological types of ADHD. One type shows *underactivation* or cortical slow-ing over the frontal region of the brain when an individual is tested on a quantitative electroencephalogram (QEEG) or with functional magnetic resonance imaging. These are the kids who can be in a classroom but totally unaware of what is being said, who read but have no idea of what they have just read, who try to write but can't think of anything to put on the page, and who are in a conversation but just "fade out." They aren't inattentive because they are think-ing about something else. They are inattentive because they aren't thinking about anything. These children typically respond pretty well to stimulant medications.

The other type of child with ADHD shows *overactivation* or cortical *hyperarousal* over the frontal lobe. These children can also be totally unaware of what is being said or what they are reading, but they are inattentive because they are thinking about tons of things. One idea sparks another and another and another. Pretty soon, they are off in their own world, thinking about things that have nothing to do with what's being said. These are the children who tend to respond poorly to stimulant medications alone. They often have some pretty significant anxiety or anger control problems and seem to be respond better to antihypertensive medications alone or in combination with low doses of stimulants such as Adderall-XR or Vyvanse.

To help identify an optimal dose of medication and to make sure it's effective throughout the day and early evening, I've found that it is useful to test the child with a QEEG. In 2013, the U.S. Food and Drug Administration (FDA) determined that such a test improves diagnostic accuracy. Studies reported by my research team and others have also revealed that this type of test helps in matching patients with medications, as well as monitoring neuro-logical response to different doses. Using the QEEG has helped us identify medication doses that ensure that the neurological causes of a child's ADHD are being treated effectively. With the FDA approval of QEEG testing for ADHD, I hope that there will be providers in your area who can offer this type of evaluation. You should be able to locate a psychologist or physician who is able to perform this type of evaluation through the websites of several professional associations (http://www.bcia.org; http://www.isnr.net; http://www.aapb.org).

HERE'S TO THE JOURNEY

So it's time for you to continue on your journey to bring out the best in your child with ADHD. Although persistence does pay off, I'm hoping that you realize that when it comes to teaching life lessons to a child with ADHD, you cannot do it alone. In the decades it took to develop, field test, and examine the life skills program presented in this book, I came to realize that the biggest missing ingredients for learning were the lack of a simple, straightforward lesson plan and the absence of a group of children to practice with. You now have a straightforward lesson plan, and if you've joined a life skills class, you have a group to work with. Hold on to some of these relationships because they will be the gateways for amazing growth in your child.

The second most important missing ingredient is effective strategies for motivating and inspiring children to persist in trying something new. I've heard it said that anyone can have a good idea, and I'm guessing that you've heard hundreds of them. What is essential in any social skills program are effective strategies for reinforcing change in a child. I am confident that the motivational techniques described in this book will serve you well in encouraging your child to change.

In writing this book, my intent is that the lessons have spoken to you in a way that you hadn't heard before, that you have learned some strategies that give you a bit more hope, and that you now have a roadmap to guide your travels and some companions for you and your child as you go forward from a place of helplessness to a much better and more rewarding place. It's a journey that you'll find well worth taking.

FINAL THOUGHTS:
A PERSONAL PERSPECTIVE

Just like you, I've been on a journey as I wrote this book. Each time I thought I was ready to complete one of my lesson plans, life happened. One of my patients would talk about a topic in a class that would change my thinking about how to teach a particular skill. One of my children would have an experience that would provide me with additional examples to use in teaching a particular lesson. Throw in a couple of floods that hit my community in upstate New York and a hurricane that hit my home in New Jersey, and it seemed like there would never be the right time to complete this book.

Each time I thought I would finally be able to complete the manuscript, some kind of crisis would hit. After a while, I simply started to accept the reality that there was apparently more that I needed to learn. I have no doubt that my experience of multiple natural disasters helped me to teach lessons on kindness, appreciation, and compassion in a much more powerful way. In a similar way, my youngest children's transition from preschool into the primary grades helped to bring home some of the realities about teasing, bullying, and the challenges of developing values.

Unquestionably, the willingness of parents and children to try out the lessons that we were teaching in our life skills classes was critical in discovering what worked and what didn't. It was my patients and their parents who were honest enough to let me know what wasn't getting "all better" despite medication, parent counseling, neurofeedback, and other kinds of treatments. The truth was that medication, neurofeedback, and other treatments may have been helping to change the neurology of ADHD, but they couldn't teach life skills. Together with my patients and their parents, we figured out a way to teach each of the skills that are included in this book. I am grateful for the persistence of the families that participated in our classes, and I hope that it paid off for each of their children.

Throughout these years, there has been an ongoing dialogue between me and my wife, Donna, about the lessons we were teaching the children in our life skills programs. My wife is the most caring, compassionate, and dedicated mental health professional I have ever met. Her ability to get to the heart of a skill and remain focused on developing a lesson that could be easily understood is greatly appreciated. I am extremely thankful for my wife's editorial perspective as I formulated each of the lessons that were developed, field tested, and eventually included in this book.

I also want to express my appreciation to Danalisa Carlson-Gotz, MA, who conducted some of the earliest field tests of this life skills program in a school setting. Although I had conducted numerous classes during the first decade of the development of this program, Danalisa was able to initially demonstrate that such a program could be viable in a school setting. Her perspective on how to translate some of my early ideas into lesson plans that could be used in a school setting was also helpful as I began to share this program with school districts across the country.

In addition, I wanted to express my appreciation to Linda McCarter, Susan Herman, and the rest of the editorial staff at APA Books. Over the years of my relationship with APA Books, I've come to look forward to the opportunity to work with such a talented group of editors. It's difficult to convey how important obtaining honest, thoughtful, focused commentary is in the development of a book. The input from Linda, Susan, and the in-house and external reviewers was extremely helpful in keeping the book on target.

Finally, it is important for me to recognize the role that God plays in my evaluation of what will work and what isn't likely to work in clinical practice. Whenever I contemplate a strategy that I am considering for use in teaching a particular life lesson or a way to motivate learning, I reflect on the lessons I've learned in the Bible. Even though inspirational books like the Bible might be confusing at times, examples of Time Stands Still, Positive Practice, Positive Punishment, and the importance of taking responsibility for our mistakes and "making amends" are found in abundance in the Bible. Trusting that such lessons came from God led me to investigate these approaches with more confidence. Looking back on the road I've traveled, I'm glad that I looked to this source of knowledge from the beginning of my work. I hope that these lessons prove helpful as you move beyond helping your child or treating attention deficits and shift to the real heart of the matter: teaching life skills to children and teens with attention-deficit/hyperactivity disorder.

SUPPLEMENTAL RESOURCES

In this section, I've included some additional articles and books to read, as well as websites that can provide additional information as you seek to bring out the best in your child or teen. Feel free to share some of your favorite resources with me by contacting me via my website, http://www.drvincemonastra.com. We're all working for the benefit of our kids. The more we share, the better it will be for all of the ones we love.

LIFE LESSON 1: SUCCEEDING IN LIFE ISN'T EASY, BUT IT STARTS SIMPLE: EAT, SLEEP, AND EXERCISE

Books and Articles

Amen, D. G. (1999). *Change your brain, change your life: The breakthrough program for conquering anxiety, depression, obsessiveness, anger, and impulsiveness.* New York, NY: Times Books.

Amen, D. G. (2013). *Healing ADD. The breakthrough program that allows you to see and heal the 7 types of ADD* (rev. ed.). New York, NY: Berkeley.

American Psychiatric Association. (2013). *Diagnostic and statistical manual of mental disorders* (5th ed.). Arlington, VA: Author.

Braverman, E. R. (2003). *The healing nutrients within: How to use amino acids to achieve optimum health and fight cancer,*

Alzheimer's disease, depression, heart disease, and more. Laguna Beach, CA: Basic Health.

Curcio, G., Ferrara, M., & De Gennaro, L. (2006). Sleep loss, learning capacity and academic performance. *Sleep Medicine Reviews, 10*, 323–337.

Fernstrom, J. D. (2013). Large neutral amino acids: Dietary effects on brain neurochemistry and function. *Amino Acids, 45*, 419–430.

Less, C., & Hopkins, J. (2013, October 24). Effect of aerobic exercise on cognition, academic achievement and psychosocial function in children: A systematic review of randomized control trials. *Prevention of Chronic Disease, 10*, E174.

Rampersaud, B. C., Pereira, M. A., Girard, B. C., Adams, J., & Metzl, J. D. (2005). Breakfast habits, nutritional status, body weight, and academic performance in children and adolescents. *Journal of the American Dietary Association, 105*, 743–760.

Sonuga-Barke, E. J., Brandeis, D., Cortese, S., Daley, D., Ferrin, M., Holtmann, M., . . . European ADHD Guidelines Group. (2013). Nonpharmacological interventions for ADHD: Systematic review and meta-analyses of randomized controlled trials of dietary and psychological treatments. *The American Journal of Psychiatry, 170*, 275–289.

Wittberg, R. A., Northrup, K. L., & Cottrell, L. A. (2012). Children's aerobic fitness and academic achievement: A longitudinal examination of students during their fifth and seventh grade years. *American Journal of Public Health, 102*, 2303–2307.

Websites

http://www.choosemyplate.gov

This is a great website that provides a lot of information about the benefits of different foods and how to develop a balanced daily food plan.

http://www.pbskids.org/lunchlab

This website provides games, information, and activities about foods. Fizzy's lunch lab is particularly fun for kids in the elementary grades.

LIFE LESSON 2: MAKING YOURSELF HEARD BY STAYING CALM

Books and Articles

Barkley, R. A. (2006). *Attention-deficit hyperactivity disorder: A handbook for diagnosis and treatment.* New York, NY: Guilford Press.

Monastra, V. J. (2008). *Unlocking the potential of patients with ADHD: A model for clinical practice.* Washington, DC: American Psychological Association.

Seligman, M. E. P. (2006). *Learned optimism: How to change your mind and your life.* New York, NY: Vintage Press.

Wilens, T. E., Biederman, J., Brown, S., Tanguay, S., Monuteaux, M. C., Blake, C., & Spencer, T. J. (2002). Psychiatric comorbidity and functioning in clinically referred pre-school children and school-age youth with ADHD. *Journal of the American Academy of Child and Adolescent Psychiatry, 65,* 1301–1313.

Websites

http://www.banzailabs.com

Offers a wide range of educational and "brainwave" apps to promote mood regulation and self-calming.

http://www.HeartMath.com

A computerized, home-based biofeedback program for teaching self-calming.

LIFE LESSON 3: GETTING WHAT YOU WANT WITHOUT GETTING INTO TROUBLE

Monastra, V. J. (2014). *Parenting children with ADHD: 10 Lessons that medicine cannot teach* (2nd ed.). Washington, DC: American Psychological Association.

Robin, A. L., & Foster, S. L. (2002). *Negotiating parent–adolescent conflict: A behavioral-family systems approach.* New York, NY: Guilford Press.

Trump, D. J., & Schwartz, T. (2004). *The art of the deal.* New York, NY: Ballantine Books.

Wantabe, K. (2009). *Problem solving 101: A simple book for smart people.* New York, NY: Portfolio.

LIFE LESSON 4: BEING CONFIDENT, PART 1: MASTER SOMETHING THAT MATTERS TO YOUR PEERS

Coopersmith, S. (1981). *The antecedents of self-esteem* (2nd ed.). Palo Alto, CA: Consulting Psychologists Press.

Honos-Webb, L. (2011). *The ADHD workbook for teens: Activities to help you gain motivation & confidence.* Oakland, CA: New Harbinger Press.

Maslow, A. H. (1987). *Motivation and personality* (3rd ed.). New York, NY: Harper & Row.

LIFE LESSON 5: BEING CONFIDENT, PART 2: FACE YOUR FEARS

Huebner, D., & Matthew, B. (2006). *What to do when you worry too much: A kid's guide to overcoming anxiety.* Washington, DC: Magination Press.

Levis, D. L. (2010). *Foundations of behavior therapy.* New York, NY: Aldine Transaction.

Prochaska, J. O., Norcross, J., & DiClemente, C. (2007). *Changing for good: A revolutionary six-stage program for overcoming bad habits and moving your life positively forward.* New York, NY: HarperCollins.

LIFE LESSON 6: FINDING OUT WHAT OTHERS LIKE TO TALK ABOUT

Karasu, T. B. (2013). *The Gotham chronicles: The culture of sociopathy.* Lanham, MD: Rowan & Littlefield.
Miller, J. C. (1998). *10-minute life lessons for kids: 52 fun and simple games and activities to teach your child honest, trust, love and other important values.* New York, NY: HarperCollins.
Shapiro, L. (2010). *The ADHD workbook for kids (Helping children gain self-confidence social skills and self control).* Oakland, CA: New Harbinger Press.
Soojung-Kim Pang, A. (2013). *The distraction addiction.* New York, NY: Little, Brown.

LIFE LESSON 7: SOMETIMES MAKING FACES CAN BE A GOOD IDEA

Carnegie, D. (1981). *How to win friends and influence people.* New York, NY: Pocket Books.
Chat Pack. (2012). *Chat pack for kids: Fun questions.* Published by Chat Pack/distributed by Etailz and Amazon.
Lowndes, L. (2003). *How to talk to anyone: 92 little tricks for big success in relationships.* New York, NY: McGraw-Hill Books
Tatum, B. D. (2003). *Why are all the Black kids sitting together in the cafeteria? And other conversations about race.* New York, NY: Basic Books.

LIFE LESSON 8: IGNORING TEASING WILL NOT MAKE IT GO AWAY

DeWolf, K. A. (2014). *Stop bullying: Effective ways to overcome bullying in school permanently: A modern day approach to prevent bullying.* CreateSpace Independent Publishing. Available at Amazon.com

Freedman, J. S. (2002). *Easing the teasing: Helping your child cope.* New York, NY: McGraw-Hill.

Wilson, M. B. (2013). *Teasing, tattling, defiance, and more.* Turners Falls, MA: Northeast Foundation for Children.

LIFE LESSON 9: EVERY DAY, FIND WAYS TO SHOW APPRECIATION

Eyre, R., & Eyre, L. (1993). *Teaching your children values.* New York, NY: Touchstone Press.

Lewis, B. A. (2005). *What do you stand for? For kids: A guide to building character.* Minneapolis, MN: Free Spirits.

Stafford, W. (2007). *Too small to ignore: Why the least of these matters most.* Colorado Springs, CO: Waterbrook Press.

LIFE LESSON 10: KINDNESS IS CONTAGIOUS

Cuyler, M., & Yoshikawa, S. (2007). *Kinder is cooler, Mrs. Ruler.* New York, NY: Simon & Schuster Books for Young Readers.

Gilbert, P. (2009). *The compassionate mind.* New York, NY: New Harbinger Press.

McCloud, C., & Messing, D. (2006). *Have you filled a bucket today?* Northville, MI: Nelson.

Rath, T., & Reckmeyer, M. (2009). *How full is your bucket?* New York, NY: The Gallup Press.

LIFE LESSON 11: ORGANIZATION IS NOT A FOUR-LETTER WORD!

For further information about the Family Educational Rights and Privacy Act (FERPA), you can contact the Family Policy Compliance Office at 202-260-3887 or FERPA.Customer@ED.gov or visit their website at http://www.ed.gov/policy/gen/guid/fpco/index.html. Mail correspondence can be directed to Family Policy Compliance Office, U.S. Department of Education, 400 Maryland Avenue, SW, Washington, DC 20202-5920.

Books

Fox, J. (2006). *Get organized without losing it.* Minneapolis, MN: Free Spirit.
Goldberg, D. (2005). *The organized student.* New York, NY: Simon & Schuster.

Websites

The following sites have a variety of great electronic tools to help a child organize, schedule, prompt, and complete tasks:

choicework (App)
http://www.dltk-cards.com/chart/
http://www.melissaanddoug.com/magnetic-responsibility-learn
http://www.motiv-aider.com
http://www.organizedhome.com
Pinterest: organizational skills for kids
http://www.plannerpads.com
http://www.smarttutor.com
http://www.timetimer.com
http://www.trackclass.com
http://www.watchminder.com

LESSON 12: PERSISTENCE PAYS OFF

American Psychiatric Association (2013). *The diagnostic and statistical manual of mental disorders* (5th ed.). Arlington, VA: Author.

Braverman, E. R. (2007). *Younger you: Unlock the hidden power of your brain to look and feel 15 years younger.* New York, NY: McGraw-Hill.

Monastra, V. J. (2008). *Unlocking the potential of patients with ADHD: A model for clinical practice.* Washington, DC: American Psychological Association.

INDEX

ABOUT THE AUTHOR

Vincent J. Monastra, PhD, is a clinical psychologist and director of the FPI Attention Disorders Clinic in Endicott, New York. During the past 25 years, he has conducted a series of studies involving thousands of individuals with disorders of attention and behavioral control. He is the coinventor of a quantitative electroencephalographic (QEEG) process that was approved by the U.S. Food and Drug Administration for use in the diagnosis of attention-deficit/hyperactivity disorder (ADHD), a pioneer in the development of parenting and EEG-based attention training procedures, and the author of numerous scientific articles and book chapters. The first edition of his book *Parenting Children With ADHD: 10 Lessons That Medicine Cannot Teach* (2005) was named Parenting Book of the Year by IParenting, and his book *Unlocking the Potential of Patients With ADHD: A Model for Clinical Practice* (2008) provides a model for comprehensive, effective, and practical community-based care for patients with ADHD. His skills as a master diagnostician and therapist have been internationally recognized and are archived in several educational videotaped programs, including *Working With Children With ADHD* (2005). He has been a faculty member of Wilson Hospital's Family Practice Residency Program; the Department of Psychology at Binghamton

University; and, most recently, the Graduate School of Counseling and Clinical Psychology at Marywood University. Dr. Monastra is the recipient of several scientific awards, including the President's Award and the Hans Berger Award from the Association for Applied Psychophysiology and Biofeedback for his seminal research into the neurophysiological characteristics of ADHD and his groundbreaking study on EEG biofeedback. He was listed among the country's most innovative researchers in the *Reader's Digest* 2004 edition of "Medical Breakthroughs." Dr. Monastra can be contacted at http://www.drvincemonastra.com or poppidoc@aol.com.

ABOUT THE CARTOONISTS

Mick Mastroianni and Mason Mastroianni hail from Upstate New York, where they keep the jokes coming at John Hart Studios. *The Dogs of C-Kennel* came to life in 2010, with Mick writing the gags and Mason drawing the characters. It has since grown to be a nationally syndicated comic strip with a great online following. This project is close to their hearts because Mason has ADD and Mick puts the "H" in ADHD. To learn more about Mick and Mason and all the happenings at John Hart Studios, visit http://www.JohnHartStudios.com.